CURRENTS IN THE

CONTEMPORARY ARGENTINE NOVEL

Currents in the Contemporary Argentine Novel

ARLT, MALLEA, SABATO, AND CORTÁZAR

DAVID WILLIAM FOSTER

UNIVERSITY OF MISSOURI PRESS, 1975

Library of Congress Cataloging in Publication Data

Foster, David William.
    Currents in the contemporary Argentine novel.

    Bibliography: p.
    1. Argentine fiction—History and criticism.
I. Title.
PQ7703.F6   863'.03   74-30083
    ISBN 0-8262-0176-8

A mi Felisinda y mi Andrenio:
ella, compañera juiciosa;
él, pimpollo ingenioso.

ACKNOWLEDGMENTS

Research for this study was supported by the Faculty Grant Program of Arizona State University. Random House publishers generously granted permission for the use of excerpts from the English translation of Mallea's and Cortázar's novels studied in Chapters Three and Five. My special gratitude to those agents of Arizona State University who have provided me with innumerable forms of indirect support in my research and to friends in Argentina who have given me assistance in many ways. Among the latter, Horacio Jorge Becco and David Maldavsky stand out as two valuable friends and scholars who have helped me "salvar las distancias."

CONTENTS

Note on Pagination of Excerpted Matter

Since many Spanish and Spanish-American novels, even contemporary works, are issued in multiple editions—rarely with identical pagination—this study cites excerpts by part and/or chapter rather than by page. Where the quotations are taken from a published translation, page references are to the English edition.

Preface

Among students of the Latin-American novel, the writers of Argentina require neither introduction nor apology: Only Mexico and Brazil can rival Argentina for leadership in the creation of Latin-American literature. Although translations into English have only now begun to attract the attention of American and English readers, the growing availability of Argentine literature in English attests to one dimension of the acceptance of these contemporary novelists.

Despite these evidences of growing interest, little in the way of analytical criticism exists for the Argentine novel, either in English or in Spanish.[1] Indeed, there is available in Spanish only the most superficial survey of the novelists; a handful of titles present the poets.[2] Thus, except for a few periodical publications and specialized monographs, the informed reader in English can turn to no general orientation for the Argentine novel, should he wish to put in focus the works that are now becoming available to him.

My purpose here, then, is to make one modest effort toward filling this great gap in our knowledge by presenting four major works by four major contemporary Argentine novelists—works that are generally accepted as cornerstones of the contemporary novel in Argentina. My discussion of the books takes the form of extended, monographic essays, for I believe that if a work is indeed important it deserves an analysis that characterizes it in detail

1. For the nineteenth century, see Myron I. Lichtblau, *The Argentine Novel in the Nineteenth Century.*
2. The most recent is Germán García, *La novela argentina, un itinerario.* Essays on selected topics are available, however, such as Juan Carlos Ghiano's collection, *Testimonio de la novela argentina.*

and demonstrates its particular significance. The result is, I hope, an effort for the Argentine novel equivalent in scope to Joseph Sommers's presentation to the American public of important contemporary Mexican works.[3] The four central chapters devoted to the principal works I have chosen to examine are couched in a framework that explains both their primary antecedents (Chapter One) and some identifiable trends of their contemporary fictional heirs (Chapter Six). In addition, I mention other works of the four principal authors. Thus, I hope that there will emerge in the reader's mind a panorama of Argentine fiction, with particular emphasis on works which may be considered major contributions that deserve special critical discussion.

In my reading, I have become aware of a stance that seems to be a constant of the contemporary Argentine novelist, a proclivity toward viewing man and his existential, sociopolitical, and cultural preoccupations in ironic terms. Sustained irony in the face of these vital preoccupations produces in the reader not only a sense of rather trivially assumed superiority on the part of the artist toward common humanity, but also, more validly, a serious questioning of the bases of these preoccupations and an exorcising, at least for the reader, of their hold. A typology of these ironic manners and of the preoccupations with which they are concerned can lead to a sociological interpretation of Argentine fiction and the national concerns which influence it, but such an approach goes beyond my interests here.

The controlling irony of some of the novels should not be taken to represent purely thematic concerns for the content of the novels. My analysis of them applies concepts derived from North-American neo-Aristotelianism and European structuralism. I shall not be rehearsing in this study the qualities of these structural orientations, but shall, rather, allow the analyses to speak for them-

3. Joseph Sommers, *After the Storm, Landmarks of the Modern Mexican Novel* (Albuquerque: University of New Mexico Press, 1968).

selves. Nevertheless, it should be noted from the outset that a concern with the ironic manners of these authors and their works is a concern with the problems of formal representation as well as with the thematics of the sorts of irony involved.

Of the four authors studied, Robert Arlt is clearly the odd man in. Not only has none of his work yet been translated into English, but many Argentine critics doubt whether it would be worth the bother. On the other hand, in the thirty years since his early death, Arlt's work has attracted somewhat of a cultist following. The cult has been expanded during the last ten years with the recognition by the Argentine new novelists that Arlt, who was a contemporary of Borges but was accused of not really being able to write Spanish and who seemed for so long to have virtually no relationship to the mainstream of Argentine literature, is indeed one of their avatars. The result has been that, with the exception of Cortázar and Güiraldes, Arlt has been the subject of more monographic studies than any other twentieth-century novelist in Argentina.

Eduardo Mallea is, in his work, the novelistic corner-stone of the liberal tradition in Argentina. Similarly to John O'Hara, he appears to have formed an Establishment canon of literary values while being roundly denounced by the dissenters, who have secured the international reputations of Julio Cortázar and Ernesto Sabato. Arlt, on the other hand, is the "find" of the dissenters, who flout the traditional values in their efforts to establish his primacy in the development of the Argentine novel. They have been to a large extent successful, and my inclusion of Arlt here is both a recognition of that success and my agreement with it.

It is assumed, for reasons stated in the first chapter, that a significant dividing point for contemporary Argentine fiction between initiatory works of limited international interest and those of indisputable and general novelistic achievement is Ricardo Güiraldes's *Don Segundo Sombra* (1926). Güiraldes's novel, although quite good by Latin-

American standards, is the last major work of the region-alistic or nationalistic vein that attracted much—though not wholly undeserved—derision here and abroad. Yet any fundamental novelistic maturity that it may possess—and contemporary criticism tends to grow more favorable—points to a final breakthrough of excellence in Argentine fiction that current novelists feel bound to uphold. To the extent, then, that *Don Segundo Sombra* is the ultimate transitional work of Argentine fiction, I have chosen to emphasize those writers who developed since that breakthrough.

This study is not a history of the Argentine novel, in the sense that to term it so implies a chronological review of novelists and their works, organized into movements, generations, and so on. It is, rather, an attempt to bring into focus works that I regard as the most significant manifestations of the genre and to give them in-depth consideration. To this extent, the novels discussed, either in terms of backgrounds (Chapters One and Six) or in terms of major works (Chapters Two through Five), must necessarily be accepted as my informed choice and personal statement concerning the literary values of this Latin-American tradition. In no way should my examination of these novels be interpreted as an effort toward presenting a panoramic history of the Argentine novel.

D.W.F.
Tempe, Arizona
November, 1974

Chapter One

INTRODUCTION TO THE ARGENTINE NOVEL

This chapter provides a brief outline of the achievements of Argentine novelists in the nineteenth and twentieth centuries. While this outline is not necessary in order for the reader to move on to the discussion of the works presented in subsequent chapters, it does indicate the nature of the fiction that was written in Argentina prior to the mid-twentieth century.

In the remainder of the study, by choosing to emphasize specific works of Argentine fiction rather than a guiding framework of traditional literary history, I have intended to provide a more detailed study of the intrinsic nature of those works than would be possible if I merely surveyed the totality of the novels produced during the last two centuries. For this reason and despite my acknowledgment of the validity of both a traditional historical survey and the underlying motivation of a committed evaluation, I propose as a profitable alternative the examination of a selected list of representative works by representative authors.[1] That is to say, following an overview of the nineteenth- and early twentieth-century Argentine novel, I shall focus on four novels by four novelists to the exclusion of other novels by these novelists or by other novelists, which might be judged as equally important. I can appeal only to the reasonableness of my evaluations as justification for my choices.

---

1. J. S. Brushwood, in *Mexico in Its Novel, a Nation's Search for Identity* (Austin: University of Texas Press, 1966), shows how it is possible to combine a panoramic survey with a framework based on Mexico as a theme in the works of that country's novelists.

The Nineteenth-Century Novel

Unlike Mexico, Argentina cannot point to a major early nineteenth-century work like José Fernández de Lizardi's *Periquillo Sarniento* (*The Itching Parrot* [1816]) as the point of origin for the regionalist, realist, and naturalist novels that flourished throughout the century. The novel as we have in general known it in the West derives its importance from its commitment to the middle-class values and mores of the eighteenth century. A Mexican work such as Lizardi's novel is significant not only for being the first Latin-American novel in any strict sense, but even more so for its promising adherence to the concerns of an emerging middle-class audience.

In Argentina, on the other hand, we search without success for an initiatory work in either the eighteenth or the nineteenth century that can be said to establish a precedent for the impressive development of the novel in the later decades of the last century. Literary historians of Argentina must be content with three early points of reference that can only with difficulty be called novels, although perhaps some basis exists for claiming that two of the documents pertain to the interests of a middle class. I refer to the early travelogues, the fiction of Esteban Echeverría, and the "imaginative essay" of Domingo Faustino Sarmiento.

The travelogues, which were written by European explorers during the eighteenth century, such as Ulrich Schmidl's *Viaje al Río de la Plata* (*Trip to the River Plate Region*, originally published in German in 1767), are given a nominal role in the development of narrative fiction because of their fantastic and imaginative tone, more proper to an exotic interest in the phenomena of the New World than to a documentary record of voyages of discovery and exploration. But aside from this rather dubious classification, one can find little direct relationship between the early travelogues by Europeans and the serious attempts to forge a national novelistic tradition in the latter part of the nineteenth century.

More intrinsically linked to the critical novel as it emerges in the latter half of the 1900s is Esteban Echeverría's *El matadero* (*The Slaughterhouse* [1838]). This short piece of fiction, a combination of essay and short story with a political point, is an interpretation of the Rosas regime in terms of an analogy to a slaughterhouse. Probably the most closely analyzed piece of nineteenth-century Argentine literature, *El matadero* is most often cited for its crude realism and its trenchant critical attitude, neither of which is particularly indicative of the emerging romanticism of the period in which it was written.[2] (Romanticism emerged late in Spain and even later in some parts of Latin America.) Romantic perhaps for its melodramatic rhetoric in the segment that constitutes the fictional exemplum, the dominant interest of the work and its black vision of Argentine society are probably better described by reference to critical principles of the Enlightenment which, despite the influence of romanticism in the artistic sphere, dominated both the Independence and later attempts to establish a democratic society in Argentina.

But whatever the textbook identification of Echeverría's work may be, its topics of interest—the Rosas government and the animalistic society it fostered—usually grant it a solid place in any examination of the development of fiction prior to José Mármol's *Amalia*. Certainly, there was no sustained attempt to produce literature of fiction in any technical sense on Echeverría's part. His composition is typical of many eighteenth- and nineteenth-century writings, in which fiction is defined by the absence of historical documentation and the presence of symbolism or allegory rather than by the complex elaboration demanded of a literary work.

Domingo Faustino Sarmiento's *Facundo* (1845) pre-

2. See Juan Carlos Ghiano's recent study, *"El matadero" de Echeverría y el costumbrismo* (Buenos Aires: Centro Editor de América Latina, 1968). Since there is an abundance of criticism available on most of the major figures cited from this point on, I will limit myself to references to one or two studies of a comprehensive nature.

sents analogous critical problems. *Facundo* is primarily an essay on the origins of Argentine society, on the background of Rosas's rise to power, and on the need to overthrow the dictator and to substitute a truly democratic society based on French principles. (It is to be recalled that Rosas did not fall until 1852, that Sarmiento was writing from exile, and that none of his ideals were realized until his own presidency, 1868–1874, the period that fostered the beginnings of a stable Argentine society.) On a less documentary plane than *El matadero, Facundo* is a skillful biography of the Tiger of the Pampas, Juan Facundo Quiroga, the provincial chieftain of La Rioja Province, whose rule of the rural areas rivaled in bloodiness Rosas's control of the capital. Sarmiento attempted to draw parallels between the two men and to use their stories to support his political principles.

The features that have most strongly attracted readers who are not primarily interested in *Facundo* as historical material is the manner in which Rosas and Facundo are evoked and the psychological understanding Sarmiento brought to bear on his exposition of their characters. Facundo in particular is presented as a highly complex individual and, as the title would suggest, his portrayal dominates the book. Although his actions may be reprehensible, Facundo is given favorable treatment because, for Sarmiento, he is simply responding unconsciously and instinctively to the deterministic circumstances of his time and place, while Rosas, the aristocrat, is consciously and selfishly exploiting a chaotic situation. It is the evocation of Facundo in these contradictory terms that is most interesting from a literary or historical point of view. Sarmiento did not hesitate to make use of many nondocumentary rhetorical devices, such as legends treated as exemplary incidents, or a general biblical invocation of damnation (the present-day wages of the sins of the Spanish conquest) and resurrection (the promised land of liberal democracy founded on the tenets of a glorious French civilization).

As a whole, *Facundo* cannot be labeled either history—in any modern sense of the word—or novel. The book is not a novel because it is an explicit treatment of political and sociological problems, which is best demonstrated via the engrossing evocation of Facundo. Despite the overwhelming bulk of Sarmientine bibliography, *Facundo* has yet to be treated from the point of view of the critical problems it presents as quasi-fiction. It continues to be included routinely in histories of Argentine literature principally for the compelling forcefulness of Sarmiento's character analyses.

The first Argentine work that can be called a legitimate novel by modern standards is *Amalia* (1851–1855) by José Mármol (1817–1871). Like the two pieces by Echeverría and Sarmiento, it too is an examination of the Rosas regime.[3] But there can be no question that, despite the documentary weight of the subject, Mármol was directly concerned with the creation of a work of literature. Nevertheless, most literary historians find themselves obliged to admit in one way or another that Mármol was unquestionably using literature for social and political ends, thus separating himself from the exclusively personal orientation commonly associated with romanticism. The factor the modern reader finds most interesting in *Amalia* is precisely the trenchant condemnation of life under Juan Manuel de Rosas.

Amalia is a novel of the terrifying conflict between Good and Evil; the often-cited cardboard quality of the characters results from each embodying an abstraction. This is particularly true in the case of Amalia; she is a stereotyped incarnation—the Madonna, the *donna angelica*—of all the traditional virtues and charms of pure woman. The same is true of the politically involved men around Amalia; they demand little more characterization than reference to Byronic figures and Browningesque

3. Concerning the fictional treatment of the Rosas period, see Harry Lee King, Jr.'s thesis, "Juan Manuel de Rosas and His Epoch as Portrayed in Argentine Fiction," *Dissertation Abstracts*, 22 (1962), 3665–66 (University of North Carolina); and Alberto Blasi Brambilla, *José Mármol y la sombra de Rosas* (Buenos Aires: Editorial Pleamar, 1970).

ideals of the relationship between a man and a woman. Amalia is cast in the role of the protector, the redemptive feminine ideal that shelters man and justifies his struggle against Evil. Evil in *Amalia* is usually acknowledged to be better portrayed and more intrinsically interesting than Good. Granted, Evil is usually more fascinating than Good, and its threat to the universal principle of Good is serious enough to engage our horrified attention.

In *Amalia*, the victory of Evil is not entirely metaphysical. Mármol, in presenting this development, is simply repeating a historical fact in a fictional context: An enormous amount of blood was spilled before Rosas was finally driven from power. Of fundamental force is the novelist's ability to make use of a historical circumstance —the long and bloody reign of terror under Rosas—as a documentary validation of a romantic vision of the struggle between Good and Evil in which the latter is by far the stronger. The triumph of Evil over Good and the reasons Mármol suggests for this triumph become, in turn, the first good example in Argentine fiction of mordant ironic manners. The inversion of the Christian formula in order to reveal the degree of spiritual degradation produced by Rosas's regime is an effective novelistic approach based on the irony of the foreshadowing of the triumph of Evil and the counterpoint of the innocent Good expressed by the young activists.[4]

Despite the bulk of fiction produced during the period that extends roughly from the fall of Rosas to the outbreak of World War I, most of it is unmemorable. This judgment is supported by the fact that, while historians of the novel find it necessary to mention most works in more or less detail, the lack of monographic studies and journal publications on the wide variety of novels reflects the unspoken consensus to channel critical interest else-

4. These comments on *Amalia* are elaborated in greater detail in David William Foster, "*Amalia* como novela gótica," in the *Actas del XV Congreso del Instituto Internacional de Literatura Iberoamericana* (Tucson: University of Arizona, to appear).

where—that is, toward the novels this study examines in depth in subsequent chapters. There are, however, at least three figures who dominate the emergence of the novel at this time, and some characterization of their work is in order. Two, Cambaceres and Gálvez, are noteworthy for having attracted a sustained critical interest.

Paul Groussac (1848–1929) was born in France and came to Argentina at the age of fifteen. Groussac is most notably remembered for heading, during the period of its formation, the Biblioteca Nacional, which was a more significant institution in his time than it is today, in its contemporary decline. Groussac's contribution to the novel is in the form of *Fruto vedado (Forbidden Fruit* [1884]), a novel of unmistakable naturalism and antiromanticism. Groussac's novel centers on a young man who becomes involved in a destructive passion of tragic and suicidal repercussions and addresses itself seriously to the problems of sexuality that were then attracting medical and psychological analyses. The novel is noted for its explicitness in the treatment of passion and introduces a bedroom-scene verisimilitude not frequently encountered in the Argentine or Latin-American novel even today. Although he used an Argentine backdrop, Groussac attempted to transcend the predominant sentimentalism of the idealistic and moralistic eighteenth century and of the pathetic and egocentric nineteenth century.

While it may be questionable whether or not he substituted the objectivity his fellow Frenchmen used to achieve "scientific naturalism," Groussac's consideration of the conflict between the values of civilization and the competing demands of the flesh is the first example in Argentina of a critically ironic anti-Establishment examination of the "underground" problems of human existence that cannot be covered up by the balance sheets of the thriving liberal economy. Part of the problem is that, with the entrenchment of a liberal economy and its attendant governmental policies there arises a pervasive Victorian morality. These standards assume an inflexible set of values and encourage the emergence of the elegant clubman. Together, these emanations assure the success of the liberal society. Argentine artists, particularly the postromantics, set out to challenge on several fronts this official view of their society, although perhaps not with the degree of devastating irony we associate with twentieth-century concepts of society that are alternative to the official ones (Arlt's and Sabato's, for example). Groussac's novel cannot, however, be called a frontal attack on the hypocrisy of liberal society. It is, rather, a supplementary vision of man that brings into focus one significant side of human nature.

The concern with problems that can be vaguely defined as naturalistic is given even fuller development in the case of Eugenio Cambaceres (1843–1888), a native Argentine but possibly even more directly oriented toward France than Groussac. Cambaceres was devoted to making an explicit case for the validity of Zolaesque naturalism (although with questionable success). His vision of the current *porteño* scene was marked by all of the cynicism and sarcastic irony of one who sees the "economic miracle" as a superficial patina of material success that obscures the underlying issues of human nature. Consequently, these vital questions lie deeply concealed and remain unanswered. Unlike Groussac's novel, which is relatively abstract in terms of a correlation between man and his conditioning society, Cambaceres's work deals with the immediate social reality of Buenos Aires. As a result, his novels capture in the language of their characters the nuances of social stratification that language can so well reflect.

Sin rumbo (*Aimless* [1885]) is an example of the Argentine's writings. This chronicle of the moral disintegration of the provincial libertine Andrés may be read on one level as the representation of the conflict between the vertiginous city and the calm, eternal countryside, with man caught between these opposing forces and their conflicting values. Andrés is unable to find "his path" and is destined to remain "aimless" in a society that demands some sort of identification or allegiance with a pattern of existence. But *Sin rumbo* is not directly the story of the lamentable confusion of value systems. Rather, Cambaceres was more concerned with a psychological portrayal of his protagonist, whose particular constellation of problems is only incidentally the result of his confusion in the face of the city–country conflict.

Both in *Sin rumbo* and later in *En la sangre* (*In the Blood* [1887]), a novel that treats the problems of the immigrant in a hostile society and his ultimate acceptance of the falseness of the promise of his immigration, no matter how we align the author with the precepts of his European models, we have works that raise serious issues concerning both the quality of the new Argentine society and its ability to deal adequately with the true nature of mankind. Cambaceres was not favorably inclined toward his characters, so he succeeded in avoiding the neoromantic sentimentalizing that appears in, for example, the Mexican Federico Gamboa's novel *Santa* (1903). Indeed, from the content of *En la sangre*, it is clear that he was critical of the official policy that encouraged foreign immigration and invited the importation of the "seeds of destruction" borne by the inferior newcomer in his blood.

Before discussing the naturalism of Manuel Gálvez, I mention in passing four novelists and their works, which fall within the context of the foregoing characterization of critical realism and naturalism in Argentina: Lucio López, *La gran aldea* (*The Big Village* [1884]), portrays Buenos Aires society during the crucial stages of its liberal formation after Rosas; Julián Martel (pseudonym of José Miró), *La bolsa* (*The Stockmarket* [1890]), a novel that questions the values of the new liberal society, with the market as a symbolic backdrop;[5] Manuel Podestá, *Irresponsable* (*Irresponsible* [1889]), an ironic work that offers in its depiction of rootless, "irresponsible" men and women trenchant marginal notes to the

5. The stock market is a symbolic backdrop in more than one Argentine work; Ernest H. Lewald, "Society and 'La Bolsa' in the Argentine Novel," *Hispania*, 43 (1960), 198–200.

balance sheets of the economic boom. Finally, I note Roberto Payró, whose neopicaresque and subtly humorous evocations of provincial life provide a delightfully understated commentary on the abyss between the "national" goals propounded in the capital and the reality these goals encounter in the rest of the country. Payró's *Las divertidas aventuras del nieto de Juan Moreira (The Entertaining Adventures of the Grandson of Juan Moreira* [1910]) brings up to date the paradigmatic figure of the rebellious gaucho, congenitally incapable of accepting either the "gifts" or the responsibilities of "civilization." Payró's Moreira, an unscrupulous politician, becomes a commentary from within liberal society on the values that threatened the original gaucho with extinction in the name of a higher civilization. Payró's fiction has aged well and continues to be delightful reading, perhaps—more than for any other quality—for its anticipation of the ironic manners of subsequent twentieth-century fiction.

The Twentieth Century Novel

Manuel Gálvez (1882–1963) is perhaps the best and the most widely known of turn-of-the-century Argentine novelists. His extensive literary career, which spanned a broad spectrum of shifting tastes and interests in Western fiction, produced some of the more readable examples of the pre-World War I novel in Argentina.[6] Given the quantity of his works, it is best to proceed immediately with a discussion of a typical novel of some excellence. Between his two most notably remembered works, the urban *Nacha Regules* (1919) and the provincial *La maestra normal (The Schoolmarm* [1914]), I choose the first for discussion.

Nacha Regules is a young woman who follows the almost archetypal road of prostitution and degradation, passing along the established routes of cruel exploitation by a pimp, attempts to achieve respectability and support herself as an abused salesgirl, suffering in the miserable

6. Myron I. Lichtblau, Introduction, *Manuel Gálvez* (New York: Twayne Publishers, Inc., 1972).

working conditions of the turn of the century, and final
resignation to the vertiginous descent to disease and death
in one house of prostitution after another, each one worse
than the previous. Nacha Regules's story would have only
a passing pseudodocumentary interest from the point of
view of this "career" if it weren't for the role of Montsalvat, the true protagonist of the novel and its controlling
consciousness. Told in the third person, it is also the story
of Montsalvat's involvement with Nacha and his attempts
to save her from her "destiny." Ravaged now by a disease
that blinds him, he is saved in turn by Nacha, to whom
he has been married two years at the conclusion of the
novel.

Who and what is Montsalvat and why is his presence
necessary in terms of defining Nacha and the socioeco-
nomic problems she represents? Nacha is easily placed by
the reader as a typical victim of the Establishment. Montsalvat, of well-placed but illegitimate birth, is a marginal
member of that Establishment. Thus, he has entree into
a world that cannot quite accept him and that he in turn
cannot quite accept for its self-righteousness and injustice
toward those of whom it must make functional and de-
humanizing use in its pursuit of "progress." Montsalvat
expounds his growing concern with the falseness of this
society in the clubs and luxurious mansions of the Buenos
Aires of the *belle époque*; he is only further rebuffed and
ridiculed. At the same time, he cannot fully participate in
the low life of the world that would have been his milieu
had his father not recognized him. The demimonde of the
compadrito—the ward boss and neighborhood tough of
the Italian quarters of north Buenos Aires—is equally
closed to Montsalvat. But it is during one of his attempted
incursions into that other world that he first discovers
Nacha, the protegée of one of the toughs. After he attempts to defend Nacha against the brutality of her es-
cort, he begins his long and pathetic search for her, a
search that merges an unmistakable sexual attraction with
a humanitarian desire to rescue one suffering individual
from an inevitable fate.

Gálvez, despite the unfortunate note of mawkish sentimentality that runs through the novel and that, in my
opinion, totally destroys the final chapters, entertains no
illusions about either the brutalizing effects of Nacha's
way of life or any practical effectiveness of liberal reform-
ism, no matter how sincere in its commitment and awareness. True, one of the characteristics of the novel is the
lack of any sustained portrayal of Nacha, who is always
seen from without. These vignettes show her accepting
humbly yet one more cruel slap from an insensitive society, which is pictured both in terms of anonymous en-
tities (the store where she works) as well as of specific individuals (the hypocritical Frenchwoman who expels
Nacha from her boardinghouse when she learns of her
past). Thus Nacha's "redemption," although effected in
great measure by the woman's obvious inner strength, is
never depicted in terms of that strength. That is, Gálvez
does not choose to report Nacha's own opinions on the
subject, which can be measured only obliquely from her
actions. On the other hand, the reader's attention is called
again and again to the development of Montsalvat's commitment toward the woman and his various decisions and
undertakings on her behalf. In this sense, the novel un-
derscores, not Nacha Regules, but Montsalvat. It is on this
basis that I have said that the novelist is more interested
in charting Montsalvat's perception of the problem and
his futile attempts to meet it than he is in portraying that
problem from Nacha's point of view.

The first work in Argentine fiction to attract wide de-
nunciatory criticism for its alleged failure to deal with the
immediate national experience is *La gloria de don Ramiro (The Glory of Don Ramiro* [1908]) by Enrique Larreta (1874–1961).[7] It is a novel that enjoys the distinction of being the first "esthetist" or decadent novel in
Argentina, the first to attract some international atten-

    7. A survey of this criticism is to be found in André Jansen, "El
cincuentenario de una gran novela: la crítica ante 'La gloria de don
Ramiro' ", *Revista hispánica moderna,* 25 (1959) , 199–206.

tion (the Spanish thinker Miguel de Unamuno wrote a eulogistic prologue), as well as the first work to establish a pattern of controversy surrounding attempts by Argentines to deal with subjects other than *compadritos* and gauchos. The novel is set in Spain (in Ávila) during the reign of Philip II (1556–1598), which is approximately the time of the founding of Buenos Aires. It chronicles with devastating cynicism the attempts of a young nobleman to attain the fame and glory promised by his time. Within this anachronistic framework, Larreta's novel serves as an excellent example of the emergence of the antihero in contemporary fiction as well as of the implication that the individual as a ridiculous failure is not endemic to our age but is a universal situation. Don Ramiro, in this sense, becomes nothing more than modern man in search of his redeeming pattern of existence, although he is decked out in sixteenth-century garb.

Ramiro's search for glory takes him through several distinct and illustrative steps, although we can in no way say that Larreta's novel is psychological despite its preoccupation with one individual's private failure. It is a novel of *telling* rather than of *showing*, to use some modern terms. Larreta tells us how Ramiro reacts and why he behaves as he does; he does not show us the inner crises that characterize his confused being. The various failures of Ramiro are measured against a Renaissance typology of success. We see his failure at religious devotion—a devotion that comes into violent conflict with a nascent sexuality. Larreta exploits this failure in order to dwell upon a torrid affair between Ramiro and Aixa, a woman of the Moorish community of Ávila who, in good decadent fashion, is revealed to be his half-sister. Having failed in religion, Ramiro attempts to pursue a career as an adventurer–politician, only to discover the dread secret of his birth: His father was a Moor who seduced and abandoned his mother. Ramiro, a bastard with Moorish blood in his veins, can have no hope of political advancement in the Spain of the sixteenth and seventeenth centuries.

The parallelism of his two failures are to be noted.

Arms and religion were the two facets of success in the Counter-Reformation period, and Larreta ties them together by the presence in his hero's background of a father who is a Moor. Ramiro's discovery of this fact is a turning point for his life, and, abandoning all hope of achieving glory in Spain, he embarks for the New World. This decision on the part of Larreta's hero gives a sort of *avant-la-lettre* validation to sociological theories that were to become current in subsequent decades as to the constitution of colonial society in some areas, notably the River Plate area, by individuals who were either escaping from an unfortunate past or who were outcasts from all levels of the mother society. Ramiro becomes a highwayman and a slavetrader and continues so until his death in Lima in 1605. We learn of Ramiro's career after the fact in an epilogue, as a novice friar explains to the holywoman Rosa de Lima (later canonized) how the sight and pursuit of her one day led to the sudden conversion to virtue and repentance of Ramiro, who dies in the beatific vision of the woman.

I think the only possible interpretation for this epilogue that would be consistent with the whole of the novel is that it is cynically ironic. It is significant that Ramiro is no longer living, in the epilogue; the story of Rosa de Lima's effect upon him is told to her by the friar as they stand beside his coffin in the church. That the epilogue is of a whole with the rest of the novel is brought out by the closing words: "Rosa de Santa María knelt piously and murmured a prayer for the soul of the deceased. And this was the glory of Don Ramiro." For Ramiro's glory to be only the prayer of a woman for his sinful and confused soul, a woman whom he had probably pursued earlier, not for her saintliness, but for her great beauty, serves to reinforce the sustained irony of the author in the face of what for him were the false ideals of Everyman as well as of his own particular time and place.[8]

8. The remarks on the epilogue of Larreta's novel are based on

Don Segundo Sombra (1926), like *La gloria de don Ramiro*, has had its share of negative criticism for both its esthetist tone and its idealistic rather than sociological portrayal of the gaucho.[9] Like Larreta's novel, Güiraldes's work has undergone significantly favorable reevaluation both within Argentina and beyond its borders. Ricardo Güiraldes (1886–1927) enjoyed the best of both worlds: As an aristocratic landowner, he was familiar with and formed by the society of the Old World, where he spent many years of his short life. But as a landowner who came to realize certain dignified virtues associated with the land, the Argentine pampa in particular, he became a defender of the gaucho and the disappearing way of life he represented. He opposed those who, following a line of social commentary initiated by Sarmiento, saw in the gaucho all that was vulgar and atavistic in American society. His novel is a defense of the gaucho and a plea for the incorporation of the vanishing values of the gaucho into the life of the "European, civilized" man like himself.

The gaucho of Güiraldes's novel, a race of men epitomized in one individual whose symbolic name, "Second Shadow," provides the title for the book, is in fact a gaucho who has had to accommodate himself with an iron will to the new realities of an organized and urban-centered society. Don Segundo Sombra is the figurative grandson of the gaucho of José Hernández's poem *Martín Fierro* (1872–1879), who is the gaucho at the moment when the emerging liberal society is attempting to destroy his kind. He is viewed as an anachronistic primitive of little value but no little danger to the "new" Argentina of the post-Rosas era. If Martín Fierro is the persecuted gaucho, in contrast to his own figurative grandfather, who

_____

my article, "Toward an Interpretation of the 'Epílogo' of *La gloria de don Ramiro*," *Chasqui*, 2, 2 (1973), 33–35.

9. Critical controversy on Güiraldes's novel is surveyed by Hugo Rodríguez Alcalá, who reflects the trend toward literary rather than cultural values: "A los cuarenta años de *Don Segundo Sombra*," *Cuadernos americanos*, No. 151 (1967), 224–55.

was the last of the triumphant gauchos of the colonial and
Rosas periods, Güiraldes's don Segundo Sombra is the
accommodated gaucho. He has accepted the bitterness he
has experienced at the fencing-in of the plains and the
circumscription of his old freedoms on the fringes of organized society, but he has not relinquished any aspect of
his indomitable character. It is this character and its rele-
vancy to the problems of modern man—who would do
well to return to fundamental rural values—that Güiraldes explores in his novel. (Compare the similar strain in
contemporary American literature from feminist writers
like Edna Ferber, Willa Cather, and Elizabeth Maddox
Roberts.)

The plot of the novel is relatively spare (it is less than
two hundred pages in most editions). The unnamed or-
phan narrator relates his escape as a youth from two spin-
sters who are raising him. He joins the gauchos who work
the herds of a ranch; he rides with them in their cattle
drives and is taken under the tutelage of the old gaucho
whose name provides the title of the work. After many
adventures and experiences that can be called "training
and maturing" for the young boy, now inextricably wed
to the nomadic way of life of the laconic and skillful riders
of the plains, he is brought back to the ranch to be told
that he is in fact the illegitimate son of the landowner don
Fabio Cáceres, who has left him his holdings at death.
The young man must now face up to his new responsibilities and accept the new role in life that destiny has given
him. Now, with his experiences on the pampas, he is more
confident in himself and able to carry out his new duties
by virtue of the manliness and character he has acquired
from don Segundo Sombra, who we assume has been
obeying a specific charge from Cáceres. The message of
the novel is clear, and as the youth laments the circumstances that force him to trade the horizonless freedom of
the gaucho for the inhibiting obligations of civilization,
his old mentor takes his leave.

Eduardo Romano, in his recent study reflecting the re-
visionary attitude toward Güiraldes, which is willing to

accept this novel on its intrinsic merits,[10] discusses in detail the *Bildungsroman* features of the novel. He calls it a novel of initiation and details with conviction the various structural and thematic aspects of the author's development of a mythic vision of a value system that is meant as a serious alternative to the dogmatic European, urban sociology of prevailing Argentine upper-class and educated society. As I have pointed out, for Güiraldes the education of the young man as a peasant without any pretensions to a way of life other than the one he has chosen by fleeing his "respectable" guardians, a way of life tied to the earth and to immutable masculine virtues of self-reliance and inner character development, points not only to the desirability but also to the possibility of a synthesis between the two dominant social classes, gaucho and landed oligarchy.

Don Segundo Sombra brings us up to the period of the Argentine novel that is the subject of this study. Güiraldes concerned himself with the values of Argentine society before most people perceived any threat of crisis. Arlt and Mallea, the two authors whose works are discussed in the next two chapters, presented their most important contributions precisely at a time when a crisis in Argentine society had indeed set in and had been recorded. As Juan Carlos Ghiano has pointed out in an observation of such all-encompassing validity as to make it nonspecific for Argentina, the Argentine novel has notably dealt with present and supposed crises. The link between Arlt and Mallea is not simply a questioning attitude toward liberal economics and society. Rather, the unity of one aspect of the novelistic tradition in Argentina after World War I is the search for viable alternatives to current values. This search forms, for one factor, the unity between Güiraldes, Arlt, and Mallea, writers who on the more specific level of vision and novelistic structure differ extensively. And we could go even further to say that the

10. Eduardo Romano, *Análisis de Don Segundo Sombra* (Buenos Aires: Centro Editor de América Latina, 1967).

unity between Sabato and Cortázar, whose works are considered in subsequent chapters, lies in their refusal to suggest alternatives and in their return to a simple critical attitude, no matter how sophisticated and ingenious the presentation.

In any case, the period contemporaneous with the publication of Güiraldes's novel witnessed the distinguished coming of age of Argentine literature in general and of the novel in particular. It would be easy at this point to list a simple cataloging of names and works along with uselessly brief characterizations of the major titles. Since this study does not pretend to fill the need for an adequate history of the Argentine novel in English, I shall make the transition to the following chapters without such a catalog. Suffice it to say, however, that at this point in the development of Argentine fiction one finds an embarrassment of riches in the form of works that cannot be ignored in a more historically oriented survey of the Argentine novel. If one adds in turn the problems created by reassessment and changes in the value of literary "stock," it will be easier to understand the task of choosing works to analyze in detail.

The selection of Roberto Arlt as subject for the next chapter reflects these issues, for it is only recently that he has received the attention his work surely deserves, although ten years ago a study such as this might not have accorded him the distinction of an entire chapter. By the same token, the works of Leopoldo Marechal (1900–1970), long the target of negative comment for his relationship with Peronism, are undergoing an impressive reevaluation and upgrading, particularly the sprawling *Adán Buenosayres* (1948), a work which manifests attempts at an ironic manner. The latter (a kind of Argentine *Ulysses*), I venture to prophesy, will emerge from current attention as either the most monumental disaster in Argentine letters or the most brilliant novel of the first half of this century.

ROBERTO ARLT was born in Buenos Aires in 1900 and died there in 1942, having lived and worked throughout most of his life within that city's lower-middle-class setting. Arlt came to literature, first fiction and later the theater, from a background in journalism that included police reporting and contact with the less agreeable aspects of city life that became so characteristic of his writings. Arlt received a measure of recognition during his lifetime, including the support of Ricardo Güiraldes, although he moved in a completely different world of international dimensions, saw in Arlt's work one viable alternative to the genteel tradition of the accepted literary circles. Yet after his death, which coincided with the rise of fascism, Arlt was as much ignored by the new populist movements as he had in life been by the upper-class writers.

The last decade, however, has seen an enormous current of interest in Arlt, who was not even listed in the Pan-American Union's 1960–1961 dictionary of Argentine authors. Both his fiction and his dramatic works have been reissued in multivolume sets under the careful editorship of his daughter, Mirta Arlt. Some unpublished manuscripts have also been made available for the first time, and several book-length studies have appeared. All of this publishing activity attests superficially to the reevaluation of the importance of Arlt during a moment of Argentine literature when the novel was not the strongest of genres, despite the quantity of titles produced. It is easy today to want to see Arlt as sharing with Güiraldes the leadership in the novel that was achieved before the international audience was later attracted by Eduardo Mallea.

Aside from any identification with Arlt by the new-leftist writers for ideological reasons, his importance rests significantly on his evocation of urban existence. The milieu of the city is evoked along with a profoundly sophisticated interpretation of its human problems—problems that, until he took them as subjects, had found only a local and limited expression in the low-class tango and *sainete* (melodrama). Where Mallea's perception of the urban reality of Argentina is eminently abstract and idealistic, Arlt's is harshly tangible, and herein lies the basis of his appeal to man in his modern, nonidyllic crisis.

*This darkness was a familiar house where he soon lost any
sense of living normally. There, in that black house, he was
used to terrible pleasures, pleasures which if he had suspected
them in another man would have driven them apart permanently.*
   *Although this black house lay within Erdosain, he would enter
through unusual and roundabout ways, using tortuous
maneuvers. And, once over the threshold he would know that
it was useless to turn back, for along the corridors of the
black house, along an only corridor always close with shadows,
a woman would move toward him with light steps, a woman
who one day on the street, on a bus or in a house had stiffened
him with desire.*[1]

One of the epithets applied most frequently to recent
generations of literati in Argentina is *parricidal.*[2] The ex-
pansion of literary activity, the international reception,
and the impressive maturity of writers during the last
twenty years or so has contributed to a parricidal rejection
by the younger writer of local forebears, particularly
those of the first half of this century. Both the writers
themselves as well as their often excessively adulatory
critics have fostered a climate of opinion which holds that
little of worth was produced prior to 1950, that with the
younger writers one can speak of a truly committed tradition of Latin-American letters, and that the public
should respect only this new establishment. The writings
of this new group are characterized by an alarmingly su-

1. All excerpts are taken from the definitive edition of *Los siete
locos* published in the *Novelas completas y cuentos,* prólogo de
Mirta Arlt (Buenos Aires: Fabril, 1963), I, 157–382. The prefatory
quotation is from p. 246 (page references are given, as the chapters
are unnumbered). All translations are my own.
   2. The epithet is borrowed from Emir Rodríguez Monegal's
study of the iconoclastic writers since, roughly, 1950–1955: *El
juicio de los parricidas, la nueva generación argentina y sus
maestros* (Buenos Aires: Deucalión, 1956). An excellent example
of "parricidal" criticism is Adolfo Prieto's *Borges y la nueva generación* (Buenos Aires: Letras Universitarias, 1954).

perficial cosmopolitanism reminiscent, not of current European and North-American letters, but of the postwar climate of the twenties.

But despite the over-all feeling among the majority of these novelists and their critics that literature in Latin America begins with them, there have been a few attempts to reevaluate the earlier writers of this century, particularly those who were unjustly ignored by their own contemporary literary establishments, writers who prefigure the concerns of the parricides. In Argentina, in addition to Jorge Luis Borges (b. 1899)—surely a representative of an earlier and most decidedly elitist tradition of Argentine literature, to whom limited respect is paid—three writers have enjoyed a reconsideration of their artistic reputations: Macedonio Fernández (1874–1952), about whom more will surely be heard in the next few years; Leopoldo Marechal (1900–1970), who achieved a distinguished reputation before being ostracized because of his support of the Peronista movement; and Roberto Arlt (1900–1942), whose untimely death ended the faltering career of a writer who is now seen as a brilliantly perceptive novelist of the human condition. Of the three, Arlt possesses the dubious distinction of having earned during his lifetime the respect of only a few fellow-writers. He was, at the same time, being repudiated with emphatic distaste by the Establishment's critical voices for both his untutored approach to the genteel profession of letters and his sympathies with (but not his active membership in) proletariat and assorted Communist/anarchical movements in Argentina.[3]

Los siete locos (*The Seven Madmen* [1929]), his most important novel, and the sequel *Los lanzallamas* (*The Flamethrowers* [1931]) are interesting precisely for their reflection of the *status animae* of the individual who, on the eve of the Great Depression, is identified with the vague underground currents of a Communist and/or an-

3. Critical attitudes toward Arlt are discussed by Juan Carlos Ghiano in his essay, "Personajes de Arlt," in his *Testimonio de la novela argentina*, pp. 169–82.

archical stamp. The antihero Erdosain, at a time when the
Argentine literary establishment is struggling to maintain
the hegemony of an official literary-supplement gentility,
becomes the first major embodiment of the flotsam and
jetsam of twentieth-century Argentine society. Erdosain
is the direct descendant of the spiritual waifs to be found
in the naturalist novel of the first antiliberal reaction in
the last decades of the nineteenth century.

It would be easy to conclude that Roberto Arlt was a
spokesman for the concerns and the objectives of proletariat socialist realism in Argentina. As far as his actual
work is concerned, nothing could be further from their
meaning. It is true that Erdosain is the paradigmatic example of the alienated man of the twentieth century, obsessed by unnamed anxieties and irremediable inabilities
to come to terms with society and existence. Within the
novel these problems are given objective status by dismissal from his job for petty embezzlement and by his
wife's cruel abandonment of him. Yet, despite Erdosain's
almost mechanistic embodiment of the features of the
perennial misfit, Arlt refuses to make him the standard-
bearer for some nonexistent or external political activism
that will neatly solve all of his problems and give him a
functioning role in the order of the universe. Such a facile
plot would produce only a work of propaganda. More significantly, Arlt possessed a spiritual alloy of Jewish and
Mediterranean cynicism that prevented him, at least as
far as his voice as a novelist is concerned, from subscribing
to romantic leftist causes. By no means does this mean
that Arlt was not sympathetic to these causes. His literature, while it cannot be easily read by a nonpartisan as
novelistic propaganda, cannot be read either as a defense
of Establishment values or as a rejection of the anguish of
the individual who did not belong to that Establishment.

Primarily at issue in Arlt's enigmatic novel is a concern
with man's dilemma that is more metaphysical than political. In this sense, it would be easy to describe him as an
existential writer, which has indeed been done often. But
either the term is too broad and ill-defined as the epithet

for any writer concerned with the problematic nature of modern man's sense of existence or it is too loosely applied to a writer who had no programmatic allegiance to the ethical idealism of existential thinkers. Arlt's concern, which he shares with innumerable contemporaries unable to discover a value system that would eradicate those anxieties, lies more closely to describing the essence of those anxieties and the curious modes of existence which they bring about. For the reader who may object that description is useless without prescription, one can only appeal to the cynical side of human nature, which denies prescriptive remedies and argues for the validity of an author's insights and their being keen enough to give adequate expression for the first time to what has since become a standardized image of man. And Arlt is all the more engaging for his capacity to maintain an ironic sense of humor in the face of the bleak, inevitable facts about man that his insights have revealed to him.

In another sense, we find in *The Seven Madmen* an impressive expressionistic conceit based on a sardonic attitude toward salvationist politics. Erdosain is the controlling consciousness of the novel, and he appears to be telling his story to some unidentified reporter who may or may not be the author. Thus, one interpretational problem is the omniscient knowledge of the narrator in the guise of information obtained from the central character. But Erdosain is in many ways less memorable than the Astrologer and his curious organization, which the protagonist joins. As the novel opens, Erdosain has lost his job, ostensibly for some petty thieving; either it doesn't matter or it's all part of an unnamed plot that, like so many incidents in the novel, is given a deliberately inadequate explanation. He then loses his wife, who seems to have seized the first opportunity to leave Erdosain. These two precipitate events, presented in a *deus ex machina* fashion that leads one to suspect either a mysterious plot against Erdosain or a deliberate undercharacterization of motivation for expressionistic reasons, lead

Erdosain to turn to the Astrologer's Society and to devote all his energies to it.

The Society, allegedly modeled after the North-American Ku Klux Klan, is a group of individuals of specialized talents: Erdosain's contribution is a special process for the electrostatic plating of flowers. The Society is plotting to take over the country and to institute a utopia based on a dictatorially imposed euphoria that will solve the problems of the citizenry and ensure absolute rule for the Astrologer and his followers. Beyond an obvious parody of Socialist–Fascist utopian fantasies then current on both sides of the Atlantic, the full implications of the Society's aims are confusing. In the first place, there are many details which the reader is not permitted to know, and there is strong evidence that the whole business is a farce mounted by the Astrologer for his own entertainment at the expense of his followers. They are a motley collection of individuals who command his interest as misfits—gullible faithful and frantic seekers after some promise—any promise—of a more perfect existence.

To the extent that one strand of Western civilization has come periodically under the sway of such promises— and the period of 1910–1940 was no exception—Arlt's conceit is essentially valid as one reasonable representation of a dominant side of human nature and only secondarily as a portrayal of specific utopian promises of modern history. Whatever the exact nature of the Society, the most important fact is Erdosain's relationship to it. Erdosain's own particular need for an order of existence that will free him from his persistent spiritual turmoil becomes the driving force of his behavior and, as a result, the narrative plot of the novel. A certain amount of attention to the Society is inevitable. There can be little question that it is a fascinating and conceitful creation, and the several unresolved questions surrounding its true nature, its actual constitution, and its real objectives make it a delightful topic of speculation. But such speculation should not detract from the central concern of the novel. To the extent that Erdosain is advanced as a controlling consciousness and to the extent that our doubts concerning the activities with which he becomes involved are also his own ignorance and naivete, a characterization of the work necessarily centers on the meaning of the individual and the rationale underlying his involvement with a project that is, from an outsider's point of view, a patently absurd and bogus operation.

A basic ingredient of *The Seven Madmen*, then, is an element of fantasy and surrealism quite disconsonant with the "committed" literature of social realism. The reader's first reaction to the novel is complete disorientation. He has little direct grasp of Erdosain as a person, since the man is presented only in vague terms of present actions and circumstances without any of the sustained background development associated with novels of character. He has even less understanding of the secret Society, of the Astrologer who directs its operations, and of the several individuals who, with their *commedia dell'arte* names and masks, are elusive faces of an elusive human order. And, finally, he has little help from the narrator, who calls himself the "commentator" on Erdosain's reportings. The narrator appears alternately to be (1) an omniscient author who organizes the entire spectacle as an expressionistic conceit on the human dilemma and man's piteous groping for a transcendent order; (2) a detached observer who favors the reader with Erdosain's comments on himself and his activities with the sect, ostensibly at some crucial point after Erdosain's *supposed* final act of involvement with the sect; and (3) another participant in the activities of the sect, part of the unnamed plot referred to above, unknown to Erdosain.

In this sense, therefore, the narrative fabric of the novel is very much a direct and maddening manifestation of Erdosain's own foggy perceptions. The reader is provided, via a few explicit comments by the narrator within the text and via at least nine disconcerting footnotes to the narrative, with some additional knowledge, such as the fact that the entire involvement of Erdosain in the sect is in the end part of an elaborate hoax against him. But essentially we remain firmly anchored to the dark glass of Erdosain's consciousness, and we experience, step by step with him, the "sense" of his anguished existence. The conceit of the secret sect is given an explicit correlation with Erdosain in the form of his specific involvement with its activities. In order to raise the basic capital with which to initiate "operations," which are to center on a chain of bordellos to provide the principal income of the Society, Erodsain is to arrange the kidnapping of a friend who can ransom himself with hard cash. After extracting the money from him, the friend is to be killed and his body dissolved in acid; the Society will at last be ready to pursue its objectives. At the last moment, as Erdosain goes to witness the execution of his friend Barsut, the autonomy of the narrative is shattered by the commentator with a footnote that provides us with knowledge denied Erdosain:

> The murderer had left the garage. Erdosain followed him, and the Astrologer, who brought up the rear, turned to look back at the man who had been strangled.
>
> Then something strange occurred that Erdosain missed. The Astrologer, stopping for a moment at the doorjamb of the garage, turned toward the dead man. Barsut, raising his shoulders as high as his ears, stretched his neck and looking at the Astrologer winked.[1] The latter touched the tip of his hat with his index finger and went on out to join Erdosain, who, unable to contain himself, exclaimed:
>
> "That's all?"
>
> The Astrologer looked at him mockingly: "Why, do you think that "that" is like it is in the theater?"

[1]*Commentator's Note:* The simulation of Barsut's murder had been decided by the Astrologer at the last minute after a long talk with the victim.[4]

What does this passage mean? The discussion that follows is an attempt to show how the novel implies a defense

4. P. 379.

of meaning as strictly an individual matter, that objective reality is indeed a farce, and that the novel, despite its often elaborate conceit and deliberate obfuscation of intent, is heuristic to the extent that it becomes a discovery experience for the reader. To whatever extent Erdosain is Everyman (hence his lack of an individuating characterization), our more or less clear apprehension of man's existential agony, through the clouded window of his consciousness, is a discovery of ourselves. Yet, at the same time, our discovery through a higher understanding of Erdosain's ridiculous objectives should serve as a commentary on our own Western religious, social, or political idealism.

The Redemptive Fantasy

The key to an understanding of the novel lies in the essential nature of Erdosain as one anguished soul who may well be a figure of Everyman. For reasons that are not made clear, Erdosain is a haunted man, a man obsessed with his own corporeal senses, with their suffering, and with some intangible spiritual malaise that has become a pervasive obsession of his existence. To a certain extent the problem is strictly social, although not in any doctrinaire sense. Erdosain is the typical by-product of an exploitive urban society, a fact most clearly shown in the opening pages of the novel when he is fired from the Sugar Corporation for petty embezzlement. It is clear that Erdosain's object in stealing the money was not to raise his standard of living, but simply to experience a few of the city's costly delights that are so inaccessible to the vast majority—a good meal, a good cigar, a good liqueur, a good movie, etc. This purpose may appear as petty as the theft itself, somewhat on the level of the waif's action when he finally manages to pilfer from the coveted wares of the candy counter. But it does become a succinct and brief correlative of Erdosain's sense of exclusion, of being an outsider, unable to participate on the most immediate, consumer-oriented level of modern life. Arlt does not belabor the point, and the novel quickly moves on to more profound disquietudes of his character.[5]

After his dismissal without charges, Erdosain returns home to confront a wife who is abandoning him for another man. One of the most depressing scenes in the Argentine novel follows. Erdosain recalls his childhood and reflects on the failure of his relationship with a woman he still loves. His thoughts are expressed in terms of sexual fantasies that were taboo in the novel of the time and that earned the author the harsh censure of genteel critics who were unable publicly to admit the existence or the significance of such preoccupations. Erdosain, then, is presented as an individual who is first and foremost the synthesis of failure, both emotional and material. Failure is the common denominator of his character, and failure has become, by the time the novel begins, the motivating obsession of his existence:

His center of pain throbbed uselessly, and he was unable to find in his soul a single crack through which to escape. Erdosain bore all of the world's suffering, the pain of the world's negation. Where in all the world could there be found a man whose skin bristled with more folds of bitterness? He felt that he was no longer a man but a wound covered over by skin, stunned and calling out with each throb of his veins.

5. There are a few direct social comments in the novel. One, on p. 194, is made by one of the members of the Society on the exploitive nature of capitalism. This point is ironic, in view of the exploitation planned by the Society in opening bordellos, but it is all part of Arlt's sardonic commentary on the designs of the group. On p. 283 the commentator observes in a note how some of the revolutionary plans of the Society became startling reality: "This novel was written in 1928 and 1929 and published by Rosso in October, 1929. It would be ridiculous then to believe that the indications of the Major [one of the "seven madmen"] have been suggested by the September 6th revolutionary movement of 1930. Undoubtedly it is curious that the declarations of the September 6th revolutionaries coincide so exactly with those of the Major, their projection being confirmed by numerous developments after the 6th of September." I cannot decide if the comment, certainly inspired by critical observations directed at the first edition, has an ironic function or is simply a true aside by the commentator as author rather than as narrator.

And yet he lived. He lived. He lived as one with the alienation and the frightening proximity of his body. He was no longer an organism brimming with sufferings but something more inhuman . . . perhaps that . . . a monster coiling in the dark womb of the room. . . . Even consciousness itself occupied in him no more than a square centimeter of feeling. The rest evaporated in the darkness. Yes, he was a square centimeter of existence prolonging with its surface of feelings the incoherent life of a phantom. Everything else had died in him, had become confused with the placenta of shadows that enveloped his atrocious reality.[6]

The bulk of the novel chronicles, often hyperbolically, this individual's almost mystical quest for a meaningful substitute for the obsessive void, for a transcendent order that will satisfy the unnamed needs of those who have been cast aside by the established order and are part of the anesthetized masses. Erdosain's problem to a great extent is his ill-focused sensitivity and anguish over the incapacity of the existing order to cope with the material and spiritual demands of most men. For those who are unaware of the dynamics of society, their lot, to which they submit, is exploitation and a dreary and stultifying existence; such was Erdosain's lot up to the moment of the novel. For those who become self-conscious the only answer is establishment of a new order that will meet directly the needs of the obsessively aware. Such an order is precisely what the Society pretends to offer Erdosain. Thus, to a great extent, Erdosain is a functional psychotic; his fantasies and his attempt to live them through the Society are a flight from the unbearable reality of an existence that is nothing more or less than the excruciating burden of day-to-day living as the vast majority of mankind knows it.

It would be uninteresting to summarize point by point Erdosain's growing involvement with the Society as it is related to the reader. It is enough to characterize both the Society and Erdosain's involvement to underline Arlt's attitude toward such transcendent orders that offer

6. Pp. 208–9.

themselves as alternatives to the admittedly destructive order of established society. The reader must absorb about two-thirds of the novel before he finally grasps the fact that the Society is a vast and brilliant hoax perpetrated by the Astrologer. Erdosain appears never to realize this falsity; to the end he is deadly serious in complying with his presumed role in a program that is to become the ultimate solution to man's dilemma. Arlt's parody of totalitarian, especially fascistic, orders is painfully apparent:

"What" [demanded the Astrologer], "is there to prevent the existence here, in Argentina, of a secret society just as powerful as [the Ku Klux Klan]? Understand that I'm speaking in all candor. I don't know if our society will be bolshevik or fascist. At times I'm inclined to believe that it would be best to put together a Russian salad that not even God would understand. I don't think you can ask me to be any more sincere than I am being right now. But note that for now what I want to do is put together a unit that will consolidate all human hopes. My plan is for us to address ourselves preferably to young bolsheviks, students, intelligent proletarians. Moreover, we can count on appealing to anyone with a plan to reform the universe, to employees that want to be millionaires, to inventors who have failed—don't think, Erdosain, that I mean to include you in this group—to anyone who has ever been fired, to people who have just been through a trial and are out in the cold not knowing where to turn. . . ."[7]

"And just what is it that you want to 'move'?"
"A mountain of inert flesh. We few want—need—the splendid powers of the earth. Blessed are we if with our atrocities we can terrorize the weak and inflame the strong. And toward that end it is necessary to create force, to revolutionize consciousnesses, to exalt barbarianism. That agent of mysterious and enormous force that will awaken all this will be society. We will restore the auto-da-fé in the plazas, we will burn alive those who do not believe in God. How is it possible that people have not realized the extraordinary beauty of these acts . . . of burning a man alive? And for not having be-

7. Pp. 182–83.

lieved in God, do you realize all this?, for not having believed in God. It is necessary, please understand me, it is absolutely necessary that a somber and enormous religion inflame humanity's heart again. Let them all fall to their knees in the path of a saint, may the prayer of the most infamous priest spark a miracle in the afternoon sky. Ah, if only you knew how many times I've thought about it! And what gives me heart is knowing that this century's civilization and misery have upset so many men. The potential madmen who cannot find their way in society are overlooked forces. In the most ignominious corner café, among two simpletons and a cynic you are going to find three geniuses. These geniuses don't work, don't do anything. . . . I'm willing to agree with you that they are tinfoil geniuses. But that tinfoil is a source of power that, if put to good use, is capable of constituting the basis for a new and powerful movement. And this is the element that I wish to make use of."

"Manager of madmen . . . ?"

"That's it. I want to be the manager of madmen. . . ."[8]

[The Astrologer] trembled as he spoke:

"We will be like gods. We will give to men stupendous miracles, delightful beauties, divine lies, we will give them the conviction of a future so extraordinary that all the promises of priests will be pale alongside the reality of the apochryphal prodigy. And then they will be happy. . . . Do you imbeciles understand that?"

All of a sudden an errand boy knocked him against a wall. Erdosain stopped in fright, clutched convulsively at the money in his pocket, and then in excitement, boundlessly happy like a tiger turned loose in a brick jungle, he spit at the façade of a boutique as he said:

"City, you will be ours."[9]

As can be seen by the distribution of the preceding extracts, information concerning the evangelical objectives of the Society is incremental. Each meeting reveals to Erdosain more of the presumed power of a new order to supplant the religious and social promises of sterile ex-

8. Pp. 274–75.
9. P. 375.

isting orders. It should be clear, at the same time, that the Society offered sardonically by Arlt is aligned with the totalitarian social gospels prevalent in the late twenties. The Society is a brotherhood, and explicit comparisons are frequently drawn by the Astrologer with the Ku Klux Klan. Man will be given a sense of belonging, an organizational and self-sacrificing identity. And this, after the nature of such evangelical operations, will provide him with the necessary fervor and impetus to involve the rest of mankind.

There is, however, a mordant irony involved here. Erdosain appears not to realize that the objectives of the Society are precisely those of the world order from which he is fleeing, which he feels has cast him aside with repulsion.[10] It is significant that the financial basis of the Society is to be the income from a chain of bordellos and that the power of the directorate is to derive from quasi-religious promises and illusions "greater than those dreamt of by any priest." Modern capitalist society has often been compared to a whorehouse in its enslavement of the unsuspecting masses for its own monetary ends, keeping the occupants dormant with meager consolations and the brutal threats of pimpish discipline. The metaphor is well known, and whether or not one subscribes to it, it is certain that Arlt—and his Astrologer—had it in mind in the sardonic and cynical creation and elaboration of an alternate order to Western society.

---

10. Erdosain can easily be called one of Ihab Hassan's "radical innocents": *Radical Innocence, Studies in the Contemporary American Novel* (Princeton, N.J.: Princeton University Press, 1961). "At bottom, all innocence amounts to a denial of death. It is, therefore, a radical plea for the Self. The plea can be holy or demonic; the Self is really the same. Deep down, where things are stark yet fearfully deceptive, man always invents his gods or becomes the gods he invents. Deep down, man always disavows the reality his hands touch and his eyes see. This too is innocence, the dangerous and outrageous kind conceived in dreams" (p. 325). Hassan is underlining the American experience in fiction, but one is confident that innumerable Latin-American innocents could recognize themselves in Hassan's characterization of an eminently contemporary dilemma of man.

For Arlt, the irony of Erdosain's circumstance is based
on his naivete, on an anguished awareness that is unac-
companied by any adequate perception of human and
social experience. That characterization may be cynical
and pessimistic with regard to Arlt's understanding of
human nature, but it does reflect the implicit conviction
expressed throughout *The Seven Madmen* that, although
man is driven by idealistic desires for meaning, transcendence, order in his awareness of himself, the answers to
those desires do not come from political and social ven-
tures such as the Society. Not that Arlt condemns Erdosain for his involvement with the absurdities of the Society. Nor does he condemn the Astrologer for the hoax
he perpetrates on the unsuspecting man. The trickery may
actually work as good for Erdosain, who suffers from an
acute case of intellectual myopia and is therefore unable
to grasp the meaning of events around him. But the question remains whether the game in the long run is adequate
even for Erdosain. It provides him with a momentary
sense of identity and importance as he goes to witness the
killing of Barsut in the name of his transcendent cause.
But his shortsightedness, his inability to comprehend that
he is only repeating in vain the gestures of the outside
world he has rejected, undermine any permanent value
for the hoax. At best, Erdosain is ignorant once again as
to his own and human nature.

As for the Astrologer, he is only pandering to the existential whims of the Erdosains among us. Arlt seems to
accept this standard justification and self-exculpation of
the panderer. The Astrologer emerges as a clever and
generous sort, willing to devote his time and energies to
the allegedly selfless fabrication of an illusion of meaning
for the life of a human derelict:

One of the Madmen, The Prospector, continued. "That's
precisely the beauty of the Astrologer's theory: men get by on
their own with their lies. He gives to what is false the con-
sistency of what is certain. Guys who have done nothing to
get anywhere, types wracked by all sorts of disillusionments,

all come to life again in the truth of his lies. Perhaps, you [Erdosain] want something even greater? Just look at how in reality that goes on all the time without anyone condemning it. Yes, everything is a façade . . . wake up to it . . . there isn't a man who won't admit the small and stupid lies that rule our society. What is the Astrologer's sin? Substituting for an insignificant lie one that is eloquent, grandiose, transcendent. The Astrologer, with all his deceits, seems to us to be an extraordinary man, and he is . . . and he is. He is . . . because he doesn't get any personal profit out of his lies and at the same time he isn't because he's doing nothing but applying an old principle used by every con man and reorganizer of society. . . ." [11]

Despite the unquestionably deceitful nature of the whole program, despite Arlt's clear rejection of both the totalitarian solution and the fabulists, one cannot help but concede its profound and therefore justifiable importance to the dupe, Erdosain. While it would be easy to condemn the Astrologer for his deceit—and Arlt's condemnation of fascism is unquestionably one of the motives of the novel—one cannot overlook the validity of the relativist principle. As Luigi Pirandello was saying at approximately the same time as Arlt was writing, with the title of a work that has become a cliché of contemporary literature, "Così è, se vi pare": That's the way it is, if you think so. Leaving aside Arlt's opinion about the Society, leaving aside the Astrologer's ambiguous motivations in directing the hoax, leaving aside our own reactions toward Erdosain's crucial blindness, we are still left with the undeniable importance of involvement, stupid or otherwise, for Erdosain himself. For this reason Arlt does not blush to elevate Erdosain to the level of a Christ figure who sees himself about to save his own soul and those of all mankind through the fulfillment of his commitment to the new order, even though that commitment involves the cruel killing of another man:

11. Pp. 293–94; cf. the Astrologer's soliloquy, which may or may not be sincere (I tend to think it is), on p. 357: "I love humanity. . . . Now I understand Christ."

The black house! I [the commentator] still seem to see before my eyes the features of that taciturn man [Erdosain] who all of a sudden lifted his eyes toward the ceiling and then lowered them to meet my own gaze. He smiled coldly and added:

"Go and tell men what the black house is. And that I was a murderer. And yet I, the murderer, have loved all beauty and plotted inside me against all the horrible temptations that hour after hour rise up from within me. I have suffered for myself, for others, don't you see?, I have suffered also for others. . . ." [12]

"Do you know? I still haven't reached the bottom of myself . . . but that crime is my last hope . . . and the Astrologer knows it, because when I asked him today if he was afraid that I'd run out he answered: 'No, not for the time being. . . . You more than anyone need this to come off so you can rid yourself of your anguish. . . .' So you see how far I've come." . . . "Now I've come to the end. My life is a horror. . . . I need to create for myself frightening complications . . . to commit sin. Don't look at me. Possibly . . . you see . . . people have lost the meaning of the word sin . . . sin is not a fault. . . . I've come to realize that sin is an act through which man breaks the slim thread that keeps him tied to God. God is forever denied him. Even if the life of that man after sin were to become purer than the life of the purest saint, he could never attain the sight of God. I am going to break that slender thread that ties me to divine charity. . . . I will distance myself forever from God. I will be alone on the face of the Earth. My soul and I, alone, just the two of us. Infinity before us. Always alone. And night and day . . . and always the yellow sun. Don't you see? Infinity expands . . . above a yellow sun and the soul that has separated itself forever from divine charity walks alone and blind under that yellow sun." [13]

12. P. 247.
13. Pp. 347–48. At this point the prostitute to whom Erdosain is speaking kneels before him, like Mary Magdalene at the feet of Christ. But, breaking the mood of the scene entirely and reinforcing once again the narrative-authorial tone of intense irony, a footnote from the commentator informs us that "Hipólita was to tell the Astrologer later that [']I knelt before Erdosain at the very moment that I got the idea to blackmail you, taking advantage of his confession of the murder plot[']" (p. 348). At a juncture

For Erdosain this is the meaning of his existence, the ultimate gesture of an empty and sterile life, finally endowed with some virtue and significance. And finally, then, this meaning must be accepted strictly on Erdosain's own terms as valid, as somehow appropriate, no matter what the "objective reality" of the situation may appear to be to the reader and to the commentator. For Arlt and for the reader, the Society may be a cruel fascist hoax to exploit the disaffected, but for Erdosain it is his own and mankind's salvation. And herein lies the novel's axis of biting irony. From the point of view of novelistic structure, we can attribute to the notes of the commentator the tension between our contact with Erdosain and his peculiar neurotic reality and our superior information about the absurdity and futility of that reality. The author shows us both the essential value of Erdosain's commitment qua Erdosain and his own sardonic skepticism concerning any universal validity for such commitments. The tension resolves itself, but only imperfectly, since the author avoids Erdosain's ultimate confrontation of his deception by the new order in which he puts so much trust. The resolution comes in terms of the reader's conclusions concerning the futility of transcendent orders, the paradox of man's quest for them, and the inescapable truth that, like his God, if they don't exist, man will create them.

I would venture to say that it is for this reason that the commentator (who may or may not be the transparent mask of the author) is reluctant to take a firm stand concerning Erdosain's adventure. The adventure is over when the story is related, and Erdosain seeks refuge because of his crime in the house of the commentator. While the host demonstrates a superior attitude and shows through his notes his own successful investigations into the actual "truth" of the events that his guest relates, he

---

such as this, one wonders who is the greater victim of a hoax: Erdosain or the reader; how does the narrator learn of the subsequent meeting between Hipólita and the Astrologer? We are never permitted to know.

confesses in the end to be as perplexed by Erdosain's character as is the reader:

> The chronicler of this story does not dare to define Erdosain, so numerous were the misfortunes of his life that the disasters brought about later in the company of the Astrologer can be explained only by the psychic processes undergone during his marriage.
>
> Even today, as I reread Erdosain's confessions, it seems incredible to me that I was a witness to such sinister revelations of shamelessness and anguish.
>
> I can still remember it. During those three days that he remained in hiding in my house he confessed everything.
>
> We met in an enormous room, empty of furniture, where very little light penetrated. . . .
>
> Impassively he piled one iniquity upon another. He knew that he was going to die, that the justice of men would seek him out mercilessly.[14]

The impact of this comment upon the reader is to shake his confidence in the facile definition of Erdosain as simply a misdirected outcast and of his confession as the babblings of an inconsequential neurotic. Somewhere between the commentator's doubts and the Astrologer's ambiguous playing at God, between Erdosain's neurotic fantasies and the reader's recognition of his own secret image, lies the central meaning of the adventure of Everyman, of this forgotten Christ. He is neither a madman nor a savior, but a complex human consciousness, and the confusions of the narrative, its points of view and its meanings, are expressionistic correlatives of that complexity which cannot be resolved in easy formulas of truth. To be sure, Arlt's critics have been consistently unable to attribute much validity to this procedure and have wanted to see in the complexities of the novelistic structure and in its unresolved conflicts the risible failures of the untutored and presumptuous writer. But more recent readers and critics are willing to see in Arlt's work, now over forty years old, early manifestations of an understanding shared by the contemporary artist that

14. P. 242.

art cannot provide answers, that it can barely provide comprehension.

Art can be content to count itself successful if it captures in its structure the enormously baffling structure of human experience. This assertion must be borne in mind and recalled when more recent works such as the novels of Sabato and Cortázar are discussed, works that are marked by the avowed acceptance of the conception of literature as a map of the unconscious rather than a program of answers to man's eternal dilemmas. Thus, in many respects in the formal, static structure of *The Seven Madmen*, the configurations of Erdosain's anguish, the details of the Society are more interesting than any narrative, dynamic structure of action and consequence. Structure is unquestionably aimless or lacking, as in the significant suppression of vital facts concerning the backgrounds of Erdosain's character and the events of his existence leading up to the opening of the novel.

The Irony of Empathy

Clearly, Arlt's novel gains coherent form from the narrator's ironic attitude toward the series of events that surround Erdosain. They are events created only in part by the man himself; more effectively, they are the shape of an absurd pattern of a marginal life with which he can identify for the first time in his tortured, trivial existence. There are several levels of irony in the novel: the irony that characterizes the relationship between Erdosain and the Astrologer's secret Society; that which involves the unnamed narrator and Erdosain (recall that Erdosain tells his story to the narrator while he is in hiding to avoid arrest for the murder which he thinks has been committed); and finally, the irony that exists between the narrator and the reader to the extent that we are denied access to any significant explanation for certain circumstances and events.

One is tempted to sum up the ironic relationship between Erdosain and the Society (specifically, the Astrologer, for the question arises as to whether the other members are, like Erdosain, dupes of the hoax or are participants in the hoax at his expense) by reference to that commonplace of contemporary thought that man is the victim of an elaborate hoax by God. In *The Seven Madmen*, the man who is playing at God is the Astrologer, who claims that he is lending mankind an important service. To the extent that mankind seeks after grandiose universal designs of existence, both theological and social, and places his unswerving faith in the meager plans available for his choice, the individual capable of conceiving and executing a truly clever plan deserves to be congratulated at least by himself. We are, however, never quite sure what the Astrologer is trying to do, and this uncertainty is part of an irony at the reader's expense. But we are sure that apparently Erdosain is completely unaware of the Astrologer's machinations.

On one level, Arlt is understandably addressing himself to the power to enchant humble and bewildered Everyman by grandiose totalitarian designs of salvation and existential meaning. On a more significant level, concerning the reasons for having as the controlling consciousness of the novel Erdosain's muddled perspective on reality, the Society becomes, not the justification of his being and the release of his tormented soul from the bonds of a degrading existence, but, quite brutally and inescapably, just another placebo administered to man to keep him occupied and mildly content until his death. There is no question that, as the novel ends, Erdosain firmly believes he has fulfilled the all-validating mission of his life; he labors under the sacrificial delusion of Christ, as the several quotations selected from strategic points in the narrative make clear.

But the reader should not, like Erdosain, be deceived. While a sense of critical responsibility usually prevents one from speculating about the development of events beyond the close of a work of literature, as though they somehow automatically achieved dynamic autonomy by virtue of their fictional elaboration in a specific work, the suggestions at several points in *The Seven Madmen* of events subsequent to the closing pages justify some tentative conclusions.

In the first place, the narrative proper is itself the *later* reporting of *later* conversations held between the narrator and Erdosain after the closing pages of the narrative, which ends with the description of how Erdosain, deceived by those who are present, goes to fulfill his destiny in the execution of the Society's hostage. Through nine footnotes, the unnamed narrator informs the reader of his opinions or of his discoveries about the events related to him by Erdosain; the discoveries obviously are made after the events. The novel concludes with the direct witnessing of Erdosain's final justification in his own eyes, shattered in ours by the narrator's footnote to the effect that the event is the Astrologer's hoax upon his dupe. Still, the reader is not permitted to take the attitude, "What does it matter that the Society is a hoax, as long as Erdosain believes that his actions and his faith have led him to a form of terrestrial bliss in the comforting arms of the redemptive Society?" Once the narrator starts telling us the extent to which his own knowledge of the events contradicts significantly the reality of Erdosain's story, any semblance of an acceptance of the man's personal sense of euphoric fulfillment must be foregone.

The only clear conclusion to be drawn from the tone of the narrator's voice and from his ubiquitous footnotes is that it is only a matter of time until Erdosain discovers the extent of the cruel hoax. This revelation must mean that, once again, Everyman will find himself confronting not only the vacuousness of his existence but also the degrading humiliation of his fateful involvement with existence. In this sense, the novel is open-ended, implying a portentous sequence of events that are only hinted at in the work. The fact is that Arlt did go on to compose a sequel to *The Seven Madmen—The Flamethrowers*. But if we limit ourselves to Arlt's vision of man as it is expressed at one point in his works, we are justified in omitting reference to the Erdosain and the Society that are portrayed in the later and equally autonomous work.

The most telling footnote alludes precisely to the events posterior to the events of Erdosain's narrative. In the satiric form of a commercial come-on, we are given intriguing promises concerning future works of fiction:

Perhaps some day I shall write the story of Erdosain's ten days [in hiding]. At the moment it is impossible for me to do so, since this book could not absorb in its pages another just as large that those impressions would demand. Bear in mind that the present memoir covers no more than three days of real activities by the characters and that despite the space available I have not been able to represent anything more than certain objective states of the protagonists, whose actions will continue in another volume to be called *Los lanzallamas* [*The Flamethrowers*]. In the second part that I am preparing and for which Erdosain gave me abundant data, there figure such extraordinary happenings as the "Blind Prostitute," "Elsa's Adventures," "The Man in the Company of Jesus," and "The Asphyxiating Gas Factory."[15]

In this way the reader is invited, if not forced, to see the effect of the narrator's actions upon Erdosain and the efficacious spell of the Society and the pseudoreligious covenant with its followers as but another more ingenious humiliation of man and his existential thirst for dignity and meaning.

Although we cannot know the exact intentions of the Astrologer, it is more important that we realize Erdosain's lack of any inkling of the plot in which he has become involved. No indication of any weakening in his faith is given in the novel, nor in his confessions to the narrator is there any hint that Erdosain is incapable of realizing that he is the victim of an elaborate deceit correlate with a vision of man as the perpetual object of such designs, divine or otherwise. Our knowledge about life, or the degree of our ability to possess that knowledge, is such that man is at best the victim of his own bewilderment and at worst the victim of deliberate hoaxes perpetrated by a being more intelligent than he. The obvious result of such thinking is that the hoaxers are in turn de-

15. Pp. 250–51.

ceived by other hoaxers more intelligent than they: Both the Astrologer and God are in turn the victims of deceit. Arlt does not explore such a potential in his novel unless it is to imply that the Astrologer's ingenious game is the result of his awareness of a higher game that he is in turn but perpetrating on even lesser mortals—he is not an astrologer for nothing.

Given this perspective on man's plight, particularly as it refers to the tragic flaw of Erdosain's veritable lust after higher meanings in the face of the obvious signs as to the nonexistence of such meanings, it is no wonder that Arlt has become a favorite author among younger writers. Along with Macedonio Fernández, and in contrast to Eduardo Mallea, who has been able to continue to believe seriously in the necessity of somehow creating meanings— a belief that does much to explain his current disfavor— Arlt prefigures the works of writers like Cortázar and Sabato. These writers reveal as a defining characteristic of their fiction this same skepticism concerning man's involvement with his transcendent beliefs, with his sterile intellectual games.

Certainly one of the major points of departure for a deeper comprehension of *Los siete locos*, beyond the facile entertainment of the absurd story, is a realization of the overwhelming role of irony in the novel and the particular form that this irony assumes at the expense of the reader, who is, after all, approaching the novel with the same naive desire to "know" that characterizes Erdosain's own stumbling contact with the "reality" of the fictional world. Once the reader grasps this ironic framework, he can never be entirely comfortable with the novel. Its barely contained tensions threaten always to produce a total disintegration or annihilation of the logical coherency that we demand of life and of its fictional representations. The structural contradictions that even the careless reader of the work is able to discover (such as the tension between the narrator's authorial omniscience vs his supposed participation in the action itself, which would then render his omniscience unacceptable) have invited serious doubts about Arlt's competence as a writer. But once we see him within the framework of Kafkaesque expressionistic fiction of the early twentieth century, it becomes easier to accept contradictions, ironies, and the lack of clear fictional autonomy as techniques metaphoric of a singular conception of reality and of its description by the literary work.

In this sense Arlt's work is vatic in its peculiar way. There is no question that Erdosain deserves much empathy from both the narrator–author and the reader. Actually, however, the narrator, in a fashion symbolic of the sensible refusal of the artist to pretend he possesses universal and definitive knowledge about man and his circumstance, confesses his own utter bewilderment in the face of Erdosain's story. In this way, *The Seven Madmen* remains Arlt's nondoctrinaire statement concerning both the plight and the failure of the common man, who is unable to entertain himself with the genteel and aristocratic deceits of other men. And, surely, there is no better "artist" than the Astrologer.

It may be that Arlt's fiction can be read as a sympathetic portrayal of those segments of society which were called, in his time, the proletariat; certainly some spokesmen for social realism in Argentina have seen in Arlt one of the few sophisticated and satisfactory practitioners of that mode. Nevertheless, one searches in vain in his novel for any prophetic message for the redemption of the classes embodied in the Everyman figure of Erdosain. Indeed, here is precisely the point of the novel: that perhaps one of the most humiliating and degrading aspects of the plight of the Erdosains is their belief in transcendent promises— whether fascistic or socialistic—that are to save them from themselves. It is true that one can fault Arlt for the absence in his novel of a viable alternative. Certainly a fundamental aspect of social realism is the injunction to offer the specific mystical goal of its own beliefs as the alternative to the preliminary identification of the unacceptable circumstances of the lower classes. But if the critic is willing to content himself with understanding the writer's accomplishment rather than in proposing ends that he might have accomplished but did not, Arlt's novel is unquestionably significant for its characterization of Erdosain as the anguished Christ manqué and for the brilliant exposition of its vision in terms of an ingenious fictional artifice.

EDUARDO MALLEA, along with the poet, short-story writer, and essayist Jorge Luis Borges, enjoys the distinction of being perhaps the most widely known Argentine writer outside Argentina. Certainly he was the most intensely discussed novelist in Argentina prior to the meteoric rise of Julio Cortázar in the last decade. Unfortunately, because of his total commitment to literature and to Argentina's agonizing struggle for national self-identity, Mallea now enjoys the dubious distinction of receiving more attention from the academic community than respect from younger writers and intellectuals. He has, in short, been one of the major casualties of the "parricide" undertaken by the post-Peronista generation.

The parricides' efforts have brought a caustic and essentially negative reevaluation of previous literary tradition that has barely spared Borges, who is Mallea's contemporary. Although Borges has survived the parricidal movement, perhaps because of his enthusiastic reception by first the French and then the American avant-garde, both he and Mallea exemplify an earlier tradition of letters centering around "aristocratic–oligarchic" publications such as Victoria Ocampo's review *Sur* and the literary supplement of the daily *La nación* (which Mallea directed for many years). One might speculate that Mallea's disfavor derives, not from his going beyond the sordid problems of the liberal society in decline, as did Borges, but from his excessive commitment to a concept of intellectual and artistic honesty that forbids the proposing of easy solutions for national problems.

Born in 1903, Mallea received a typically elitist education, marked by early repeated trips to Europe. One of these visits, in 1934 on the eve of the European disaster, may be said to constitute an autobiographical basis for *La bahía de silencio* (*The Bay of Silence* [1940]) , the novel I discuss. His early publications, beginning with his second book in 1935 (the first is a 1927 collection of short stories), *Conocimiento y expresión de la Argentina* (*Knowledge and Expression of Argentina*), reflect from the beginning of his career his preoccupation with his nation's growing dilemmas and the position of the intellectual toward them. As has often been said, Mallea's fictional characters are the thin masks of their author, although this statement does not impugn the literary quality of the novels and short stories. Mallea has published an extensive list of books, too many to list here and many of which could be called excessively long. He is best known for the 1940 novel I discuss here, the autobiographic work, *Historia de una pasión argentina* (*History of an Argentine Passion* [1937]); *Todo verdor perecerá* (*All Green Shall Perish* [1941]); *La torre* (*The Tower* [1951]); *Simbad* (1957). In the concluding chapter of this study I mention Mallea's more recent works. He continues to reside and write in Buenos Aires.

That I for por auld Scotland's sake
Some useful plan or book could make,
Or sing a song at least.[1]
But there is a rapid life and a slow life. The slow life we live
within ourselves, far from the swift, external one. The slow
life stores up in us strange, deep cravings, fatigues, and
aspirations—as the poet Whitman said—to meet the night, storm,
hunger, ridicule, accidents, and rebuffs as calmly and unperturbed
as the trees and the animals. "Passive, receptive, silent." That,
and what it deposits within us is the foil to so much artificial
agitation.[2]

Prior to the most recent generation of Argentine writers, only two novelists had attained what can be called
a truly international stature: Ricardo Güiraldes and
Eduardo Mallea. Güiraldes's recognition outside his native country was probably due less to intrinsic artistic
merit than to a romantic, exotic appreciation for his evocation of a unique but fading way of life. As to Mallea,
we might also suspect that at least the initial awareness of
his works could be attributed to his reputation as an
essayist concerned with the increasingly apparent failure
in the thirties and forties of Argentine economic and social institutions. As Martin Stabb has pointed out,[3] Mallea as an essayist belongs to that group of writers who,

1. Quoted by Mallea in English from Robert Burns, Ch.
XXXIX, *La bahía de silencio*.
2. *La bahía de silencio*, Ch. XXXIV; Ch. 33 in the English
translation, p. 194. This following edition is used: 4th ed. (Buenos
Aires: Editorial Sudamericana, 1960). Unless indicated, excerpts
are from the English edition, *The Bay of Silence*; translated from
the Spanish by Stuart Grummon (New York: Alfred A. Knopf,
1944). It should be noted that Grummon abridges the novel by
about 50 per cent.
3. Martin S. Stabb, *In Quest of Identity: Patterns in the Spanish
American Essay of Ideas, 1890–1960* (Chapel Hill: University of
North Carolina Press, 1967), pp. 159–69, 172–73, in Ch. VI, "Argentina's Quest for Identity."

during the period between the two World Wars, attempted to raise fundamental questions concerning the national and spiritual goals of their countries.

One answer offered by Mallea to the questions raised has become his most famous and his most controversial. Writing at a time when Western society was torn between the ideas advanced by socially-conscious, Marxist-inspired literature and those of various modes of psychological literature that contributed to the excruciating self-consciousness of existential writers, he took a strong position with regard to the role of the intellectual, and this stance was bound to evoke heated debate. Mallea's disfavor with more strident elements of the Latin-American literary world can be traced to the position he early assumed in his analysis of the Argentine question. Taking exception with the tenets of social realism and adhering more closely to the insights of the psychological novel, Mallea came to assert that a national reality in general and Argentina in particular could be spoken of in terms of the *visible* and the *invisible*. The visible is the observable social, cultural, political circumstances of the country and its citizens; the invisible is the psychological basis for the observable reality, seen both in terms of the forces of national history and in terms of its unspoken values and beliefs. The visible is the sham of modern man, driven by crumbling values that can only be considered false; the invisible comes to be represented by the individual who is aware of himself and of his society, the individual who accepts the potential for spiritual evolution and who accepts its inevitability if mankind is to enjoy any meaningful existence. Mallea's writings around this theme include the essay *Historia de una pasión argentina* (1939) and his subsequent fiction. Both genres evoke this dichotomy and delineate the individual who will assume the role of the "invisible Argentine."

Fiction as Commitment

The Bay of Silence (*La bahía de silencio* [1940]) is Mallea's most significant fictional representation of his con-

victions concerning the need for citizens who will revi-
talize national ideals. An immense, sprawling novel that
at times appears to be formless, essayistic, and sentimental,
The Bay of Silence traces the steps of one individual, a
flimsy persona of the author, as he evolves in his role as
an invisible Argentine. Martín Tregua's evolution, which
spans some twelve years, hinges on internal Argentine
events during the years following the Great Depression.
Although the city is recalled with a detail common to the
Argentine novel, the social, economic, and political background is rarely if ever referred to directly. The author
depends on either his reader's general familiarity with
these circumstances or his willingness to accept the anxiety of the "lost Argentine generation" of Tregua and his
associates as indicative of the spiritual milieu of the invisible, if not the visible, Argentine.[4]

Tregua's retrospective memoirs—for this is the nature
of five hundred pages of the novel—are divided into three
parts: the man's youth as a student in Buenos Aires and
his association with a group of men who edit a magazine
of literary and general sociointellectual commentary; Tregua's hadji to Europe, the Mecca of all affluent and educated Latin Americans, in an attempt to explore the
bases of his national society, and his discovery that the
Old World is even more decayed and bankrupt than the
New; and finally, Martín's return to Buenos Aires during
the closing years of the thirties, the so-called infamous
decade, as a successful novelist of the national crisis, his
failure to solve the emotional crisis of a lover, and his
resignation to being little more than a withdrawn but
committed individual adrift in a "bay of silence," satisfied
if he can bear witness to the context of man and to his role
as an invisible Argentine. It is at this point in his evolution that Tregua decides to write the memoirs that constitute the novel. He dedicates them to an unknown
woman whom he feels, in her silent suffering and grief, to

4. On this view of Mallea, see Fred Petersen, "Notes on Mallea's
definition of Argentina," *Hispania,* 45 (1962), 621–24.

be a fellow invisible traveler in the chaotic morass of their visible society.[5]

It would be far too easy to study the *The Bay of Silence* as little more than a slightly fictionalized essay. Perhaps one of the potential weaknesses of a work of literature is the ease with which commentators can treat it as essentially an essay and overlook with little embarrassment the elements of novelistic and esthetic structure. There can be little doubt that Mallea, whether because of the distinction of his convictions concerning fundamental questions of the Argentine national character or because of a fatal weakness in his fictional expressions of these convictions, has been studied all too often in terms of his contributions to the intellectual currents of Latin America.[6] This essayistic emphasis is a characteristic of Mallea's fiction, and it influences the critic's approach even when his work is discussed in terms of literary history. It represents, perhaps, the inherent danger in being both a good novelist and a good essayist. Whatever the case may be, *The Bay of Silence* has inspired less than acceptable criticism as literature.

If one is disposed to quarrel with the approach assumed by previous commentaries on the novel, he must be equally disposed to suggest the intrinsic qualities of the work that argue for a critical evaluation of the novel that goes beyond its intellectual content. In other words, what has the novelist done to ensure that his work is read primarily as a novel? Five features deserve special attention in support of the contention that *The Bay of Silence* deserves closer analysis from an intrinsic point of view. It is no accident that these features match dominant charac-

5. H. Ernest Lewald characterizes the novel in these terms in his article, "Mallea's Theme in *La bahía de silencio*," *Hispania*, 40 (1957), 176–78.

6. This is essentially the approach to all of Mallea's works taken by John H. R. Polt, *The Writings of Eduardo Mallea*. Despite chapters on "Characters," "Structure," "Literary Style," Polt sees the fictional works as essayistic, and accordingly he treats them from a predominantly ideological point of view. Stabb, however, resists the temptation to correlate essay content and fictional creation.

teristics of the North-American and European novel of the period.

First, the work is set within expansive boundaries of time and space. Rather than being satisfied with the relatively simple and straightforward evocation of his central thesis, Mallea presents a complex of motivating ideas in the personal terms of a well-defined character who evolves over a period of time within contexts that stimulate an interplay between his acute consciousness and his surroundings. The length of the novel argues against any facile conceptual basis on the part of the novelist. Critics who search for the ideas of literature to the exclusion of structure and general literary elaboration overlook a fundamental factor: the *raison d'être* for the form of the work. An initial justification for the length of Mallea's novel lies in the need to present an extensive, *personalized* elaboration of his convictions. Such an elaboration is possible only via a fictional structure in which the author is able to create the illusion that his characters are functioning as they would in real life, that the ideas they articulate stem from their experience with life. The point, then, is to demonstrate how these ideas can be the actual experiences of an autonomous personality and not just the disembodied projections of an inaccessible essayistic voice. The novel is a form of art that seeks to prove through the performance of its characters within a real circumstance *how* man arrives at the beliefs, convictions, motivations, behaviors that can be attributed to him. This is a rather superficial observation about the nature of fiction, but it seems to be frequently overlooked by Mallea's critics.

The elaboration of form in Mallea's novel, a purportedly verisimilar, pseudobiographical world, derives from the author's effort to impress the reader with the artistic niceties of a novel. One finds it difficult to believe that, with the effort involved in executing a novel—even a bad one—a writer can be indifferent to the demands of literature. There are, however, readers of Mallea who have been willing to dispense with the fictional edifice in order to concentrate on the essay supposedly contained within. The essayistic is undeniably there. No respectable claim can be made for a literature totally devoid of ideas or convictions, but a valid distinction is to be made by the critic between the work's expression as an essay and its infinitely more complex and subtle expression as a novel. It is precisely for this reason that I disagree strongly with Shaw's harsh judgment of *The Bay of Silence* for not arriving at any positive, constructive conclusions.[7] We might make this demand of an essay or of a quasi-essayistic tract meant to move men to action. But as a novel, Mallea's work can no more be judged in these terms than can any "pessimistic" work of literature (such as, to give two contemporary examples, the novels of Pío Baroja and Ernest Hemingway). Further, it is difficult within the framework of modern literary criticism to construe novels as calls to action. While moral interpretations and evaluations gauge the correspondence or lack of it with the values of the reading public, the critic who imposes strictly pragmatic criteria on a novel both demeans the expressive nature of literature and raises doubts about the right of the novelist to render an honest characterization of his vision—ambiguous and pessimistic or otherwise—of the human circumstance.

A second major feature of *The Bay of Silence* that affirms strongly its artistic intention is the nature and role of the narrative voice. Martín Tregua is telling his own story, the story of an individual who, no matter how exemplary or symbolic he may ultimately be within the ideological structure of the work, remains unmistakably an individual. The work assumes the form of a *Bildungsroman* because of Mallea's desire to chronicle in detail the development of Tregua as a singular, if messianic, invisible Argentine.[8] And, by having Tregua speak in his own

7. Donald L. Shaw, "Narrative Technique in Mallea's *La bahía de silencio*," *Symposium*, 20 (1966), 50–55.

8. Despite Tregua's subsequent doubts, Mallea's protagonist would certainly exemplify William R. Mueller's definition of a novelistic prophet: "Historians of the human spirit—prophets, if not evangelists and apostles—who, following earlier prophetic

voice with his acute self-awareness, Mallea not only underlines the importance and necessity of an unmistakably existential and ethical commitment on the part of both author and character, but also demonstrates the novelist's
decision that the narrative voice contributes to the fictional, novelistic nature of the work. The result is to suppress
all authorial comment—often a disadvantage in a work
based on intellectual premises in that the author may find
it difficult to avoid essayistic commentaries that detract
from the vital drama of his characters. Although the
character may himself indulge in discussions, stream-of-
consciousness meditations, arguments articulated with
himself, these essayistic digressions nevertheless remain
firmly associated with an individual as an integral part of
his personal experience. The omnipresence of the first-
person singular in the novel is in marked contrast to the
anonymous and depersonalized voice of the essayist, who,
no matter how impassioned his point of view may become, typically strives for an illusion of intellectual objectivity in order to enhance the universal validity of his
personal beliefs.

Mallea is not content just to give his work an unmistakably novelistic structure. In order, one supposes, to
justify Martín Tregua's introspection and to provide a
credible outlet for his almost exaggerated preoccupations, Mallea makes Tregua a writer and a novelist. On
one level it would be easy to match Tregua's novelistic
endeavors with Mallea's and to insist that the latter's characters barely escape being merely convenient masks. But
this would be too facile for the novelist as well as for the
critic and would imply that Mallea is incompetent, both
as a novelist and as an essayist. The logical consequence
would be to speculate as to the value of producing a work
that purports to be a novel if one is interested only in producing thinly veiled autobiography. While there are un-

voices, analyze and chronicle the sickness of their own civilization
and, at times, chart the narrow redemptive road." *The Prophetic
Voice in Modern Fiction* (New York: Association Press, 1959),
p. 24.

doubtedly many aspects of *The Bay of Silence* which are clearly autobiographical, beyond any assumed convenience to Mallea in his portraying Tregua as a novelist concerned with the essence and quality of national existence there lie some other more subtle reasons.

First, Mallea is able to imply that there is a serious aspect of his work through identifying himself and his character as novelists. This interior duplication, whereby the concept of a work of literature becomes one motif of the novel, is quite common in contemporary fiction.[9] In both Mallea's novel and in Sabato's *On Heroes and Tombs,* we find as part of the narrative texture of the works a preoccupation with the nature and limitations of the novel. In Sabato's work, these considerations focus on the refusal of the modern novel, because of the impossibility, to explain life to the reader. The fictional illusion is that the reader must content himself with the raw material in order to discover through his own efforts the underlying patterns and explanations. But we find in Mallea a more traditional reliance on the novel as a tentative vehicle for portrayal and explanation. That is to say, Mallea adheres to an essentially classical concept of literature in which the reader may be "instructed" through the representation of fiction.

Nevertheless, while adhering to the principle of literature as a means of awareness and education, the interior duplication in *The Bay of Silence* becomes, on a level beyond the simple autobiographical portrayal of Mallea as a writer, the representation of the difficulties of fiction.[10]

9. Leon Livingstone discusses some Spanish examples in "Interior Duplication and the Problem of Form in the Modern Spanish Novel," *PMLA,* 73 (1958), 393–406.

10. I strongly suspect that a good case could be made for the importance of this internal concern of the novel with its own nature, although I can offer only scattered Latin-American examples at this time (various works by Carlos Fuentes, Gabriel García Márquez, Joaquín Gómez Bas, Ernesto Sabato, Julio Cortázar, Gustavo Sainz, and others). Although D'Lugo speaks of "self-conscious" form in the novel, his abstract indicates that we are not talking about quite the same thing: Marvin Alan D'Lugo, "Self Conscious Form: The Perception of Reality in Contemporary Latin Ameri-

Thus, the novel should be read as both an expression of Martín Tregua's preoccupations over the crises of the thirties in national and Western society as well as a representation of the dilemma facing the individual who wants to communicate artistically his concern to others. In this sense, *The Bay of Silence* relates three separate frustrating attempts at communication in addition to the primary relationship of the novel to us, the "real" reading audience. I refer to Martín's difficulty in expressing himself, a difficulty that involves, first, the people with whom he comes in contact in the inner circles of Buenos Aires intellectuals and with whom he engages in dialogues in the course of his maturation. From the point of reference of Martín's own voice, that is, the story he relates—the world of his inner anxieties and concerns—remains essentially cut off from the rest of the world. Both the realities of day-to-day living as well as the artificialities of café dialogue prove to be, as the modern novel is wont to repeat, inadequate to the task of meaningful communication.

It is an awareness of this unbridgeable chasm that causes an individual to turn to art, supposedly an invincible means of communication. First as an essay writer for magazines and intellectual reviews, later as a widely recognized novelist who re-creates in his fiction the agony of the times, Tregua seeks to discover an even more powerful outlet for the articulation of his witness. Throughout the latter part of the novel Tregua is involved in a disastrous and pathetic affair with a woman whose spiritual crisis he attempts to solve through his ultimately ineffectual concern and affection; he is concurrently writing a long novel, *Las cuarenta noches de Juan Argentino* (*The Forty Nights of John Argentine*). The novel (whose title is probably a reference to God's wrath over the degeneration of mankind) is in ironic counterpoint to his failure to touch the life of the woman whose presence represents his

can Fiction" (Ph. D. dissertation, University of Illinois, 1969). See also David William Foster, "*La región más transparente* [by Carlos Fuentes] and the Limits of Prophetic Art," *Hispania*, 56 (1973), 35–42.

personal side. It is at the point that Tregua realizes that both novel and affair have been delusions, that he is prevented by the limiting nature of communication from affecting the lives of others with his actions and writings. As a result, he writes the pages that become Mallea's novel.

Tregua's memoirs are addressed to an unknown woman, a woman whom he does not pretend to affect and who will probably not even read the work. For Tregua, that woman, whose life he has followed from a distance over a long period of time, fascinated by the inner tragedy which she projects, is also trapped in the "bay of silence." He sees the two of them as concerned with the inner self of man, unable to bring about the awareness and the spiritual renovation necessary for building a decent society, and resigned to the agony yet inner strength brought by the acute self-awareness that can be a person's only lasting "conquest." Because of the obvious nature of the novel as Mallea presents it to us, we are privileged to witness the private one-way communication between these two invisible Argentines. Nevertheless, it is clear that Tregua's decision to abandon the fiction that has brought him fame yet left him unsatisfied in his self-appointed prophetic role implies his realization that it is virtually impossible to achieve an effective "prophecy" through the artistic medium of literature. An inescapable consequence is that we must acknowledge Mallea's desire through this interior duplication to make us aware of his doubts concerning the value of this work of fiction.

Perhaps one of the most curious aspects of Mallea's novel is the form of personal address used in order to provide a coherency of perspective as well as to emphasize the status of the work as a personal memoir that we, the "real" readers, are privileged to examine. In order to demonstrate the tone of the work and to substantiate many of the observations made up to this point, I have transcribed a long quotation from the novel. In this passage Martín Tregua dedicates the work to this unknown fellow invisible and suffering Argentine. The intensity of the personal note at this point should be noted, along with the sentimentality that is an unfortunate characteristic of many of Mallea's works. Perhaps it is justifiable here because of the personalized circumstances of the passage:

I stand with those who await the final triumph, safe together in the bay, in the bay of silence.

Think of the fact that in this city and in this land, which we have loved so much and for which we have loved so much, our full measure of zeal, of passion of blood has been given and that that is a good enough contribution, like the land that becomes moist and produces in its crops the quality of certain species. Oh, if only this were idle boasting! Can one boast of misfortune?

All I'm doing is telling you that this misfortune does not belong to us. That it is simply there and that what you do when you give it is share it.

I can't keep myself from being sententious. It's a sign of certain types of fatigue. But tomorrow morning when I wake up, I'll be rested again, working on other stories that will also have a destination, even though anonymous, stories that I hope will not end up lost. But if they do become lost, they will at least have had some purpose, because they can't be deprived of what I've given them: blood.

I have cut my life down to its most elemental forms. At times I go out to see the dawn over Buenos Aires and at other times I don't go to bed without having seen her beautiful nocturnal sky. I see only simple people, very simple people. I'm becoming more and more withdrawn inside myself, and I've almost gotten to the silent heart of the country.

When I was a young boy, my father, whom I go to see every now and then for a few days' rest, used to tell me the story of the man who never put his head in water to wash it, but who would use his hands to pour water over it. This man who refused to put his head in water to wash it was always dirty. That water seemed to me like life and it doesn't do any good to splash around only on the surface. You've got to be drowned once and for all and to go on facing up to your own deep waters, refusing to avoid yourself by any of the ready evasions available.

Perhaps you and I will never meet, or perhaps we will meet

some time. That all depends. But there is something which is certain. We will know that we have fought it, that we have gone on, that we are still here. But, what a relief to feel that our share of blood has already been given, the encounter a sustained success! I won't say defeated. For me the word defeat is unimportant, or at least when it refers to external and conventional triumphs.

You have no idea how much it would please me if this account—and how somber, monotonous, and insistent it is!—were of some use to you. Nighttime conversations are that way, insistent, belabored. But they don't leave us anything more to say, and we can only go out to meet the morning, knowing. . . .

I've been with you for a long time while writing these memoirs, and it's time now to take my leave. I'm alone in my room, with the windows shut, and it's late and it's all over.[11]

One's reaction when he first discovers that the narrative is an open letter to an unknown woman is to attempt to justify the procedure. Why not write the novel from the first-person point of view without addressing it to anyone, which is certainly the most customary technique in the confessional novel? If Mallea's intent is indeed to state in a well-constructed fictional form his concern for the quality of Argentine and Western life in the thirties, it would seem natural for his work to be the direct self-characterization of the protagonist. The reason for the procedure used, then, must be more than the curiosity of it. One does confess to *someone*, someone other than the reading public, which, by the conventions of the traditional autonomous novel, is nonexistent within the closed, hermetic world of the work. Since the novel is not addressed to the "dear reader" to whom Tregua might plausibly owe a frank and unreserved confession, any question as to why and to whom he feels compelled to bare his soul is resolved in the shadowy person of Señora de Cárdenas:

11. Ch. XLIX. The translation is my own; the fact that the English translation omits the concluding pages of the novel raises serious questions as to whether the translator understood it.

It was that terrible interior prey of yours, that terrible and proud intimacy, that cold and reserved haughtiness that attracted me to you irresistibly. All that was secret, solemn, somber and grandiose in the world seemed to me hidden in that unyielding, aristocratic withdrawal, in that jealous pride.[12]

All this is hard to say, but perhaps easy to understand. I am sure that in one way or another you too have sought it around you. The most dramatic thing in the world is that search, in others, for the justification of what we carry within us in our most innermost being, that something that is both the most disconsolate and the best.[13]

Yet such a characterization is an unsatisfactory explanation of the decision to use a second-person addressee. Nor does it account for Martín's strange attachment to this distant figure, whom he has purposely avoided meeting and who is unaware of his "pursuit of her existence."

A much more important reason, I feel, has already been given: Tregua's failure as an intellectual in the sense of an individual witness and as a particular kind of novelist. Although his interest in the woman extends back to his early years as a student, the decision to abandon the novels that are his established form of expression and to undertake the memoirs is essentially an admission of failure as a witness and as a writer. Recognition that both his life and hers have brought them to a dead end, a refuge in the "bay of silence," may be infuriating to the social activists who read Mallea's novel, but it is a hard-won realism for Martín Tregua. For Tregua, the turning away from the dialogue of personal interrelations represented by his day-to-day contact with fellow human beings and by his involvement with those to whom he owes a personal commitment (his intellectual colleagues of the first part of the novel, his Belgian doctor-friend of the second part, and the woman whom he attempts to "salvage" in the third part) and his rejection of the witness he has served

12. Ch. II; my translation (not included in the English translation).
13. Ch. II; my translation (not included in the English translation).

publicly in his writings can be taken only as an implication of his awareness of the inadequacy of his mission as a man and as an artist:

Sometimes it is not a voice that speaks in us but an ownerless emanation as old and impersonal as the complaints of the lower classes and the ambitious tone of the upper. It was not my voice that spoke in me. Suddenly it became a cry: "No one influences anybody. No; no one influences anybody!" The check boy handed me my hat as I was leaving the restaurant. "Thanks." No; no one influences anybody.

The September sun bathes the street and the baroque façade of an old residence—someone did not see it—and the display of glassware in the show windows of a prominent store. My mouth was tightly closed, but the voice inside broke out in a mad burst of laughter: "To influence! To influence! What a coarse satire life is!" Who exerts influence? There are casual and accidental influences, but who can influence deliberately? . . .

Here is Santa Fé Boulevard. The new church is wedged between two apartment houses; where were the sacred love and inspiration of the architect to give it the indescribable atmosphere of Santa María Magdalena dei Pazzi or even of the colonial Santo Domingo with the heroic balls surmounting its humble towers? I went inside. It was so long since I had been in a church. I remained standing in the gloomy nave, troubled by the liturgical rhythm that flowed spontaneously from the few pale, tapering lights burning before the titular saint. I offered not a tear or a vocal prayer, only that pain, and desolation at our inability to influence human acts by persuasion or conviction.[14]

Despite the unpromising implications of Mallea's novel, *The Bay of Silence* is not totally pessimistic about the prophetic role of the social novelist. The existence of the novel, despite any internal renunciation of fiction, announces Mallea's implicit belief that it can and will serve some good. Thus, it should not be difficult for the informed reader to make the fundamental distinction between the attitudes attributable to Tregua through the novel and any conclusions to be drawn concerning the

14. Ch. 55 (pp. 328–29) of the English translation; Ch. LVII of the original.

potentially quite differing views of Mallea himself. They may be identical, but then again they may not be. And publication of *The Bay of Silence* would suggest some belief in the expressive validity of fiction as opposed to Tregua's sentimental conclusions to the contrary.

The characteristics of Mallea's *The Bay of Silence* dealt with here underline convincingly the overwhelmingly novelistic nature of a work that is too easily examined only as a lightly fictionalized, autobiographical essay. The most effective argument for a basically literary approach to this work is the privateness and the sentimentality of the memoirs. Both of these features suggest that the narrative is intended to be taken as the anguished expression of an individual who, constructively or otherwise, has come to a realization that is directly at variance with the active public role he had attempted to play in the course of his adult life. It may be that Tregua's realization does not seriously contradict Mallea's convictions concerning the "invisible Argentine." But both privateness and sentimentality underscore, at the expense of intellectual considerations, the fundamental novelistic status intended for the work.

The Narrator as Prophet

Despite the foregoing considerations concerning the relationship of *The Bay of Silence* to Mallea's essayistic writings and its implications concerning the social functions of literature, the novel remains essentially a *Bildungsroman* that revolves around the spiritual development of one individual and his agonic role in human society. Despite the focus of the novel on a single personality, there is little doubt that some sort of special relationship exists between Martín Tregua and his social circumstance. It is not simply that Tregua is intended to be a symbol of Argentina or of one aspect of Argentina. Indeed, one point to be made, either for Mallea's essays or for the narrative structure of this novel, is that Tregua is atypical of an Argentina of visible citizens who are, like most men, more actively concerned with economic gain than with the discovery of solutions to the spiritual needs of mankind. As I have pointed out, Mallea's novel is set during the period of the decline of the liberal economic institutions established in the country during the latter part of the nineteenth century. Responsible for the spectacular growth of the country that entitled Argentina at the turn of the century to be considered the United States of the Southern Hemisphere, capitalist leaders were secure in their conviction that economic solutions were, in fact, social and, by implication, spiritual solutions.

Notwithstanding the similarity of his beliefs to Marxist economics, Mallea's protagonist in *The Bay of Silence* would have us understand that mankind must satisfy the aspirations of mind and soul along a different axis of achievement. To be sure, it is this dual repugnance for both capitalism and Marxism that caused Mallea to be viewed as an outsider among the intellectuals of earlier decades of this century. Unable to accept the value system of the dominant conservative-liberal persuasion, he has been likewise unable to sympathize with the socialistic movements that the Establishment has considered its greatest enemy. One aspect of the novel concerns his contact in Belgium with a group of refugees from the growing Fascist tide in Europe. Although not really Marxist, their collectivistic views, which are bewildering to the Argentine, are those of the humanitarian activists so easily identified with the romantic Internationale of the thirties. It is significant that the group meets in an old, decrepit theatre to discuss and to plan their program. For Tregua their drama appears pathetic. The American can no longer look to Europe for intellectual and spiritual guidance: "They were the fragments of a Europe that was changing, traveling unexplored, incredibly rough paths." [15]

15. Ch. 38 (p. 231) of the English translation; Ch. XXXIX of the original. I prefer for accuracy the translation, "They were the remains . . . ." One is tempted to speculate on how Mallea might have viewed these men had he, when he wrote his novel in the late thirties, had any idea of the eventual consequence of the Fascist tide.

Part II of *The Bay of Silence* is titled "Las islas" ("The Islands") and can be taken as referring to both the isolation of the lost souls of those who were destroyed by the Depression in Europe (Tregua's Belgian doctor-friend is a representative figure here) and the inescapable sense of aloneness that descends upon the mature and sensitive individual. Tregua's European interlude, between the youth of Part I ("Los jóvenes" ["Youth" or "The Adolescents"]) and the bitter disillusionment of Part III ("Los derrotados" ["The Defeated"]), marks a turning point in the development of his awareness, stimulated by the clarity of vision afforded by his absence from Buenos Aires. In Europe Martín Tregua is able to realize, first, that his own anxiety is not unique and can be attributed to a universal awareness of the essence of life that became more obvious with the decay of the thirties. He realizes, second, that his concern for the spiritual crisis of issues concerning the struggle for the renewal of social values, for the individual's attainment of emotional and intellectual self-awareness, is a problem of international consequences. It is this realization that gives Tregua a broader understanding of his commitment. He is now able to return to Buenos Aires and to comprehend his own and his country's place in a universal dilemma.

Mallea's novel is therefore both psychological and social, but both in restricted and unique ways. In the first place, the reader who demands an in-depth characterization of Tregua along the psychological lines of Freud, Bergson, and other popular currents of the postrealist novel will be disappointed. Throughout the five hundred pages of the novel Tregua remains essentially ephemeral, incorporeal. In part this circumstance is due to Tregua's narration of the novel in his own voice, which allows for the portrayal of only the most immediate levels of his consciousness. Any deeper levels of consciousness cannot be portrayed directly and must be either inferred by the reader or represented by the author through the self-revelations of an unsuspecting narrator. Neither approach appears to be valid for the purposes of this novel, for

Mallea's interest is not in how or why Tregua came to possess the introspective sensitivity which is the basis of his anxiety and concern. Rather, emphasis falls again and again on the greater importance of the individual's ability to grow spiritually with the consciousness that, as if by accident, he has come to possess.

Tregua, therefore—and this is a major aspect of the novel—is not interested in searching back in time to discover the roots of his psyche. Although his story is retrospective, his interest lies always with the definition of the development of his perceptions in the present. Far from being a rounded, fully-developed character, Tregua's personality as it is presented in the novel is defined exclusively in terms of a motivating commitment and a resigned awareness. From the point of view of character development, Tregua is singularly unsatisfying, and it is as incorrect to read Mallea's novel in terms of psychological portrayal as it is to so read *Beowulf*. For both, the goals of the narrative are different and the manipulation of character is therefore different. It would seem that Mallea's intent is for Tregua to be neither symbolic nor allegorical; otherwise the *The Bay of Silence* would be a slightly fictionalized essay, and there are too many arguments against such an evaluation. It would seem better to accept the presence of Tregua as he is presented to us: as an agonizing, disembodied intellect and as a representative of the sort of community envisioned by Mallea.

Beyond the question of the psychological aspects of Tregua's portrayal, his special relationship to society makes the novel undeniably social in implication. Tregua accepts voluntarily a self-conscious role of prophetic identity. Part of his commitment implies the willingness of the individual to become a witness for the renewal of society as a whole:

... a center capable, through the soundness of its position, of polarizing those in the nation of good will, men with a sound and courageous intelligence. Most important of all was establishing a point of contact. With an island you can build a continent. Not a debate society but a center made up of

people able to go out and seek the truth wherever it may be
and to speak it with sufficient courage and candor. Why can't
we set up an island where we can begin to breathe the air?
What a community can use are the guts and the faith, the passion and the strength of a few.[16]

Eschewing sacrifice in terms of the flamboyant Christ-
figures of many of the novels of the thirties, Mallea evinces
a concept of martyrdom that is reduced to the humble
willingness to accept in the name of humanity the torment that comes with the acute awareness of existence.
From the point of view of Tregua's agony as it is presented in the closing pages of the novel, it might as well
be as public a martyrdom as that of the sacrificial fugitive
in Ignazio Silone's christological *Bread and Wine* (1937).
Certainly, the object of such a sacrifice is not the whole-
sale resurrection of Argentine or Western society. Rather,
as in John H. R. Polt's synthesis, it is "the elevation . . .
of human life to the sacramental level, and the demand
that man make of his life something valuable, something
of a temporal greatness. . . . This greatness cannot be
achieved without suffering. Through suffering we gain
extension and depth, and are made aware of the reality of
others, and are brought into communication with them
on the plane of intelligence and love."[17]
It is because of this existential suffering of a man for
himself and for others that his life may attain greater
dignity and purpose through self-awareness that I have
spoken of Tregua's commitment as that of a *witness*. Tregua's vision is of a humanity that is passive rather than
visible, vocal, active. This fact has led to the two-pronged
attack on Mallea's fiction in general and *The Bay of Silence* in particular to which I have referred. In the first
place, on an ideological level Mallea clashes with Western
militant radicalism, also concerned in its best manifestations with the social and spiritual quality of life. From

16. Ch. XL; my translation (not included in the English translation).
17. Polt, p. 33.

the points of view of both the leftist militants of the thirties and those of the New Left of today, Mallea's passive,
quietistic solution is far from acceptable.

As for esthetic considerations, Mallea's passive, inactive
characters like Martín Tregua have invited harsh criticism for their lack of kinetic development. For many
readers, they simply do not move or accomplish enough
to be considered sufficiently autonomous characters. That
is to say, Martín Tregua throughout remains a nebulous,
ethereal person, individuated by the nature of his con-
fessed thoughts, anxieties, and commitments rather than
by his realistic interaction with other men and with his
immediate, tangible surroundings. On one level, we can
easily dismiss these detractions of the novel for its lack of
adventure and its overemphasis on Tregua's inner consciousness. Any criticism based on such factors is ingenuous at best. However, for those who would defend the
essential fictional quality of *The Bay of Silence*, comments such as the following by Polt, based on doubts as
to the literary value of Mallea's fiction,[18] are more difficult
to dismiss:

Whether this character [Martín Tregua] really embodies
the ideas which he is supposed to represent is made questionable by discrepancies between his life and thought. Tregua
stresses the importance of intangible and transcendental values as against superficial physical appearances. Yet he main-
tains for some time a relationship with . . . a woman opposed
to all his theories of love and self-surrender—but an attractive
woman. . . .
    Tregua for all his insistence on the necessity of communi-
cation, fails to establish a lasting emotional relationship with
even one person. His connection with the Señora de Cárdenas
is a highly abstract and onesided relationship of which he
alone is aware. In the realm of national problems and national regeneration, also, Tregua's actions contrast with his
speeches. They consist, in fact, only of his writings. His novel
does not seem to have any effect; his newspaper is a failure,

18. Cf. Polt's skepticism on p. 91 in the conclusions to his
study.

the men who organized it disband, and Tregua loses or avoids further contact with them. . . .

In sum, the character Tregua is unreal, inconsistent, and static. His situation with respect to his unsolved problems is exactly the same at the end of the novel as it was at the beginning. He acquires an illusory reality from the interesting ideas he discusses with such fervor; but an analysis of him as a character reveals not Martín Tregua but Eduardo Mallea. The disguise is too thin to establish Tregua as a creature capable of independent and authentic life.[19]

It would be difficult to counter Polt's statement concerning the relationship between Tregua and Mallea. It is predicated on the widely accepted novelistic premise that, if there is meant to be a one-to-one correspondence between author and character, it should not be obvious. A corollary assumption—reduced to a matter of taste, in view of current trends in the novel—is that the characters of a novel should indeed possess "independent and authentic life." However, even if one were readily to accept Polt's criticisms concerning the ephemerality of Tregua as an autonomous character, the opening portion of the passage quoted is far less acceptable. One of Polt's difficulties with *The Bay of Silence* seems to be his failure to realize the importance of identifying the narrative voice with Tregua and the circumstances of his failure of communication. That Tregua is "unreal, inconsistent and static" is a double-edged criticism: it may be lamentable either from the point of view of an unrealized novelistic endeavor, *or* it may be an aspect of the human nature that Mallea, by design, has attributed to Tregua. The first alternative is clearly Polt's assumption, and if the critic can assume that Tregua should be real, consistent, and nonstatic or that Mallea failed in his wish to characterize him in this fashion, then the judgment is damaging.

Mallea emerges from Polt's study as a writer with a strong commitment to such a concept of literature. It is all the more significant that in *The Bay of Silence*, supposedly the most typical expression of his ideology, he

19. Polt, p. 62.

should create a character who is obsessed with his successive failures to communicate his urgent preoccupations. In ironic terms, we see the character not only as a supposed projection of the author but also as a powerful symbol of despair over the inherent weaknesses of literature as a pragmatic form of communication. Thus, the inadequacies of Tregua *as he presents himself to the reader* become, not the inadequacies of Mallea's novelistic craft, which must be judged on other terms, but the dismal inadequacies of the individual whose novel ideals to move a nation clash glaringly with his limitations as an all-too-human individual. These are, then, the underlying reasons for the "discrepancies between his life and thought."

The importance of *The Bay of Silence* lies both in the role of Martín Tregua as a witness and *vates* for a particular type of human commitment and in the portrayal of that role through the fictional representation of Tregua's own confession of failure and despair. The commitment, as many critics have recognized, involves a unique sacrifice and self-awareness in order that the individuals of society may attain a greater dignification and fulfillment of human existence. To an extent, some parallels can be drawn between this commitment and the goals of Sartrean existentialism. The fictional representation, on the other hand, emphasizes the fundamental inadequacy of man by nature to realize even the most meager advances in this commitment. Told as a flashback and as one man's agonized confession of failure, the novel contrasts dramatically with any objective formulation of that commitment. From the point of view of a novel written as a literary work of art, both the role of the narrative voice and the subsequent contrast are inconsequential. Tregua's story cannot avoid being colored both by his own telling of it and by the nature of man's vague and confused memory.

The Bay of Silence may well have been conceived as the fictional representation of an intellectual preoccupation with Argentina and Western society, originally expressed in influential essays. But there can be little doubt that, in the realization of this fictional expression,

Mallea has made the far more important artistic contribution of implying a perception of the inherent limits of
intellectual–spiritual commitment and its pragmatic formulation as literature. The "bay of silence," in addition
to being the situs for the despair of failure and for the resigned passiveness of a tenuous hope in a distant fulfillment of the invisible society, becomes also the realm of
silence that the novelist must realize subconsciously he is
doomed to inhabit: "How beautiful and deep the bay is.
There is where those who have made a triumph out of
their failure can be found. There, now, there the bay of
silence awaits you and them. And I see you all there, silent
and waiting." [20]

20. Ch. LIX; my translation (not included in the English
translation).

ERNESTO SABATO* is basically an unknown man in his private life, despite his recognized importance among contemporary Argentine and Latin-American novelists. Indeed, his life (he was born in 1911) presents one outstanding anomaly: In his early manhood he held both teaching and research positions in physics, yet renounced science out of the belief that it promoted a rational concept of man which is radically at variance with human experience. Since the late thirties and early forties, Sabato has devoted his creative efforts exclusively to literature.

Although Sabato has written numerous essays, his novelistic production is limited to the short novel, *El túnel (The Tunnel* [1948]) , published in English as *The Outsider* in 1950, and the two sprawling masterpieces, *Sobre héroes y tumbas (On Heroes and Tombs* [1961]) and *Abaddón, el exterminador (Abaddon, the Exterminator* [1974]). His principal collections of essays are *Uno y el universo (One and the Universe* [1945]), *Hombre y engranajes (Men and Cogs* [1951]), and *El otro rostro del peronismo (The Other Face of Peronismo* [1956]). *El otro rostro* is perhaps the first assessment of Peronismo to be written after the fall of Perón in 1955; the Peronista "experience" serves as the shadowy backdrop of the 1961 novel.

Unlike Cortázar or Borges, men constantly in the public eye, Sabato cultivates the obscurity afforded by the bureaucratic and private positions he has held over the years. The impression is that he rather effectively flees the attention of literary coteries, a fact that may account for his reluctance to release any of the fiction he had written since *On Heroes and Tombs* until the publication in 1974, some thirteen years after his second novel, of *Abaddon*. Indeed, the latter novel, which continues many of the motifs and techniques of *On Heroes and Tombs*, gives an initial impression of being an assemblage of fragments written autonomously over the period of a dozen years. Nevertheless, a first reading of the novel indicates that it will contribute to the solidification of Sabato's importance in the new Latin-American novel.

*Throughout this study I follow Sabato's decision to remove the accent mark from the first vowel of his name.

Little by little Bruno came to find out about certain things, bits and fragments, through those interviews, those absurd and at times unbearable meetings. Martín would start speaking all of a sudden like an automaton in jumbled sentences, as if searching for something like the delicate track on the strand of a gale-swept beach. They were, moreover, the fragile tracks of phantoms. He was seeking the key, the hidden meaning. And Bruno ought to know, had to know.[1]

Although he is a prolific essayist, Sabato is acclaimed for a comparatively small output of fiction. Only three novels form the basis of his literary prestige: *El túnel* (*The Tunnel* [1948]); *Sobre héroes y tumbas* (*On Heroes and Tombs* [1961]); and *Abaddón, el exterminador* (*A-baddon, the Exterminator* [1974]), which was published as this study was being prepared for publication.[2]

The first is a novelette rather than a novel; in barely 125 pages the protagonist relates his weird tale of murder —the gist of the book. A work of Freudian obsessions and Sartrean alienation, *The Tunnel* has received an almost excessive amount of critical attention. These assessments have been, however, limited in view. Numerous papers have focused on the Freudian and Sartrean aspects, which may appear rather worn to today's knowledgeable reader; little attention has been paid to Sabato's technical skill in

1. Part IV, Ch. II of *Sobre héroes y tumbas*, in his *Obras de ficción* (Buenos Aires: Losada, 1966), pp. 153–724. All translations are my own from this edition. The reader should note that later versions of the novel show some significant changes from the original edition, Buenos Aires: Fabril, 1961.

2. The best study to date on Sabato is Ángela B. Dellepiane, *Ernesto Sábato, el hombre y su obra*. See also Fred Petersen's competent dissertation (although the 1961 novel is barely touched upon): "Ernesto Sábato: Essayist and Novelist," *Dissertation Abstracts*, 24 (1964), 2910 (University of Washington). Harley D. Oberhelman has also published his useful survey, *Ernesto Sábato* (New York: Twayne Publishers, Inc., 1970).

creating a central ambiguity. To what extent are we to believe the confessions of a psychotic murderer? Most critics have implied that there is no question of the narrator's reliability while they overlook the relationship between the narrator as a troubled painter and the author as a troubled artist. Both struggle, ultimately in vain, to express the total hallucination of their obsessive personal vision of the hypersensitive artist who cannot cope with an excruciating self-consciousness. Although commentators have failed to describe this aspect adequately, Sabato appears to have proposed the fundamental dilemma of the sensitive artist, the romantic *Aussenseiter*: He sees and he sees all too profoundly. This privileged perception not only sets him off from normal life but becomes also the major stumbling block to the realization of his creative efforts. In *The Tunnel* the result is the inability to continue painting. Further: The dilemma of the artist is to become one of the central unifying forces in *On Heroes and Tombs*.

On Heroes and Tombs is virtually impossible to categorize generically. Ostensibly one novel, it is actually a work that incorporates the drafts of several autonomous narratives. Its four parts, rather than fitting into any traditional format of development, create a vast panorama from several narratives that can be taken as a total image of Argentina. Perhaps, if it is necessary to classify the novel, it could be called an *anatomy* in Northrop Frye's sense of the term.[3]

In a sense, one story is told several times. It is the story of the despair of sensitive individuals confronted by an irrational and degrading existence, their quest for the roots of that despair and for a release from the lofty absurdities of the collective "glory" of their society. Like Oliveira in Cortázar's *Hopscotch*, the several characters

---

3. See Northrop Frye, *The Anatomy of Criticism* (Princeton, N. J.: Princeton University Press, 1957), pp. 302–14. Frye uses the concept *anatomy* to characterize modern intellectual modes of fiction, as opposed to more individual-centered forms such as the confession or the traditional novel.

of *On Heroes and Tombs* are trapped in the labyrinth of their personal awareness of a spiritual malaise. But where Oliveira becomes merely another absurdity within the absurdity, Sabato's pathetically earnest characters do not provoke ironic bemusement. Brought up in a culture that pays extensive and often excessive homage to its national heroes, Sabato incorporates into his novel a brilliant interplay between the supposed glories of the past and the putative decay of the present (the closing days of Peronismo), between the gothic secrets of an impoverished founding family and the daily battle for survival of the lower-middle-class masses, between the "seers" whose personal and national vision leads only to spiritual impotence or dangerous hallucination and the "blessed ignorant" who, in their acceptance of life, are able somehow to go on living.

As a grab bag of a novel, *On Heroes and Tombs* can be grasped only as an abstract collage,[4] and its narrative richness serves to focus the work as a profound statement on modern man trapped between his illusions and his anxieties. Although in *The Tunnel* the only reasonable outcome can be homicidal lunacy, in Sabato's second novel, which he claims to be an antidote to the bleakness of *The Tunnel*, we find the unmistakable attempt to conclude with a positive perspective. Emerging from the four narratives to define the novel as a fictional totality is the clear movement from the vacuous glories of the past to the rugged fraternal promise of the new frontiers of the present.

The past is represented by General Lavalle's famous and disastrous March to the North in 1841. It is observed in all its stupidity and meaninglessness through the eyes of a Lieutenant Olmos, a forerunner of the illustrious founding family whose destruction is one aspect of the

4. To appreciate how much Sabato's novel is a complex, it is instructive to study Dellepiane's schematic representation of the themes and subthemes of the novel (p. 196). Where I have spoken of the novel as exemplifying Frye's *anatomy*, she speaks of its *Baroque* quality.

novel. The new promise of the present, the boy Martín, finds the solution to his adolescent sense of emptiness in a journey to the South, to the vast regions of Argentina, which remain to be settled and populated. In his decision to undertake this trip—the acceptance of a possibility open to him from the outset of the novel—Martín faces a new future with resolution. He puts behind him the web of strange events in which he has been caught for two years without his merely normal intelligence ever having been able to understand the circumstances he was both privileged and cursed to live through.

Martín, the boy who suffers, is the son of "la madre cloaca," the Mother Sewer—his term for his selfish mother and the vulgar and degenerate middle-class society she epitomizes. Martín is an adolescent whose less than superior intelligence means that he is dazed by life most of the time. Yet Sabato makes him the one unifying consciousness of the novel. That it is Martín rather than, say, Bruno, the frustrated novelist who is the confidant for Martín's outpourings of confusion, fear, and despair, underlines the novel's focus. Rather than on the abnormal, overintelligent individual of *The Tunnel*, the novel centers instead on his more normal counterpart. Martín, typically, is bothered for a time by the growing pains of adolescence. As a result he is led to the abyss of the total annihilation that consumes the artists and intellectuals, although in the end he achieves the emotional and spiritual equilibrium of a man who has unconsciously but unmistakably arrived at a viable truce with life. As the poets and clairvoyants of the novel meet their self-wrought apocalyptic end, Martín sets out in happy camaraderie with his new mentor, a truck driver, to discover the new frontier. For North Americans who have lived through the demythification of the Winning of the West, Sabato's depiction of Argentine historical myths may seem overly sentimental. But it is necessary to read the novel in Argentine terms, in which the demythification affects the heroes of the Independence, in which the ideal of the frontier is not yet reduced to the clichés of television, and, most significant, in which poets and intellectuals have traditionally presumed to be the chosen few who interpret the problems of existence. For Sabato's novel, it is precisely this group's concept of superiority that becomes the source of so much human suffering and destruction over the span of five hundred pages.

The Anatomy

The novel is divided into four parts. Part One, "The Dragon and the Princess," relates the initial meeting and subsequent erratic relations between Martín and Alejandra. They meet suddenly one day as though she had planned the encounter, and throughout their ensuing relations Martín cannot escape the sensation that there is something planned and deliberate, something that remains persistently beyond his grasp, that is the basis for the most peculiar boy–girl affair in Argentine letters. Alejandra is the "princess" of the title; the "dragon" is the power that lies within her, the unknown, subconscious forces that keep her soul in constant and tortured turmoil. Poor Martín, excruciatingly innocent, attempts valiantly to cope with Alejandra's fits, with her hallucinations, and with her smiles that become shrieks of terror. But he is no Saint George, and he only begins to uncover the secret of Alejandra's personal hell. The reader is permitted somewhat more information, although it is still sketchy: The girl is held under an incestuous spell by her father, Fernando Vidal, a man of stunningly evil cynicism. Unable to free herself from this state, Alejandra seeks refuge in Martín's innocent arms in an affair that, on one level, reads like a story in a pulp magazine. Alejandra seeks escape also in ritual acts of purification with first water, then the fires of her nightmares, and finally the real flames in which she immolates herself and her father. The first part of the novel ends with Martín's realization, following one of the girl's especially frightening seizures, of how deep indeed is her disturbance:

"Martín," Alejandra said with a weary voice, "I'm very, very tired, I need to sleep, but don't leave. You can sleep here at my side."

He took off his shoes and lay down beside Alejandra.

"You're a saint," she said as she cuddled up next to him.

Martín felt her fall asleep immediately. He tried to order the chaos of his spirit, but it was all such an incoherent whirlpool. His thoughts kept coming out so jumbled that, little by little, he was overcome by an uncontrollable drowsiness, by the sweetest sensation despite everything of being beside the woman he loved.

But something kept him from sleeping, and little by little he was overcome with anxiety.

It was, he thought, as if the prince, after having crossed vast and desolate regions, were to find himself in front of a grotto where she slept, watched over by a dragon. And it was as if, to make it worse, he were to notice that the dragon did keep vigil at her side as we usually imagine in childish myths. But, and this was even more unsettling, that he was inside of her: it was as if she were a princess–dragon, an indiscernible monster, pure and flaming at the same time, innocent and repellent at the same time: it was as if the purest child in a Communion dress had nightmares of reptiles and bats.[5]

Part Two, "The Hidden Faces," relates Martín's attempt to cope intellectually and emotionally with the little he has discovered about Alejandra and their increasing alienation as she and her father, each by their own separate paths, which the reader is never privileged to see cross, prepare themselves for the final act in their hideous drama. The "hidden faces" are the unknown forces that Martín, for the first time in his life, perceives as chthonic emanations that beleaguer man. Although the novel is hardly a *Bildungsroman* on the psychological maturation of an adolescent, one can speak of Martín's "initiation" in his growing awareness of the depth of these forces with which he in part becomes involved. However, for Sabato the hidden faces are not only the individual's inner devils; they include as well forces that harass man on a collective or national level.

5. Pt. I, Ch. XVII.

It is no accident that the father and daughter's self-imposed destruction takes place on the night that was crucial in the fall of Perón's dictatorship. While the two are meeting for the last time before their death, Martín is rescuing religious statues from the churches being burned by Perón's enraged supporters. Thus, two purgings by fire take place, one representative of the decline of the founding families, which Perón's regime had so viciously attacked, the other represenative of the last gasps of a Fascist government based on the mass rule of the lower-class thug. Symbolically, all that remains are the puzzled Martíns of the broad middle class, presumably the new hope of Argentina in their sense of fraternal responsibility, their lack of overintellectualism, and their self-conscious freedom from the brutal selfishness of the supposed "shirtless" masses. Martín, in being just a "nice," sincere, suffering individual, stands out in the end in unconscious relief against the background of the Peronista disaster and the tableau of human waste that was the life of Alejandra and her father.

On Heroes and Tombs is decidedly representative of the expressionistic new novel. Existence does not yield itself to neat explanations and decipherings; the novelist is not a god who holds the key to ultimate divine revelation, but is merely a tormented seer. Indeed, Sabato's novel rests on nothing more than the elaboration of a spurious newspaper report on the homicide–suicide of the two paranoiacs.[6] The novel, the elaboration of the journalistic

6. The prefatory note is presented as a fragment from the police columns of the 28 June 1955 issue of *La razón*, an actual Buenos Aires evening tabloid of proletariat identification. It is interesting to note that the first edition couched the report in a commentary by the narrator. The absence of his overt presentation of the news item in subsequent editions removes him from the novel as the "historical" narrator, although throughout we realize that the novel is presented as a report by someone to whom the events it relates have been told. Thus, there is no omniscient point of view that permits unrestricted access to the characters' psychology. It is due in large measure to this fact of structure that Alejandra's inner torment remains so remote and unspecified. To understand her father, we at least have his own writings (see Part III of the novel).

note, the "human-interest story," may be rich in detail
and in the narrative representation of human behavior,
but it is not much more explicitly informative. The
reader is left, like Martín, unable to fit together all the
myriad pieces and fragments into a pattern that makes
convincing sense.

The second part of the novel ends with Martín's stupe-
fying discovery that the other man in Alejandra's life is
her father, and he secretly follows her to their final ren-
dezvous. At this point, for both the reader and Martín,
the threads of the narrative, rather than coming together
in a coherent synthesis, spread apart. Instead of explanation and understanding, both the reader and the controlling consciousness of the novel are left in mystery and
confusion.

A Memorandum on Truth

Part Three is a further diffusion of so-called novelistic
economy and unity. In this, the longest segment of the
novel (it runs to over 130 pages), the reader is presented
with Fernando Vidal's "Memorandum on the Blind," ostensibly an account of his attempt to get to the heart of
the "Sect of the Blind," which he is convinced rules the
world. Vidal's memoir is part diary, part confession, part
exposé. Vidal's premises concerning the underground
movement of the blind, which exerts an absolutist influence on the destiny of both its members and the normally sighted, are patently absurd. He goes to hyperbolic
lengths in his conclusions, with the result that this part
of the novel stands apart as an autonomous document
and has been for most readers perhaps the work's most
memorable feature. Nevertheless, so much interest has
lain in justifying psychoanalytically Vidal's scribblings
that not enough attention has been given their relationship to the novel as a whole, a relationship the critic must
assume it has, if he is to justify its inclusion in the work.

The document is without doubt a brilliant piece of
"confabulation." Sabato has taken a person who is only a
shadowy presence in the first two parts of the novel, who

materializes physically only for Martín to discover that he is Alejandra's father, and has provided him with a psychological characterization of true creative talent. The memoirs are incredible for the extremes to which Vidal goes in his hypotheses concerning the master plot of the blind. Claims of persecution like Vidal's leave the normal person wide-eyed with the relationships, interpretations, prophecies they advance, all based on an incredibly faulty reasoning. In Sabato's novel, Vidal's hypothesis is spellbinding as a magnificent flight of fancy: the blind men who sell collarstays and shoestrings in the subways are spies (surely they could never live on what they sell—the most exaggerated need for collarstays could not support one of them!); the agents of charitable institutions for the blind are really representatives of the Sect who establish contact with potential new members in order to enlist them in their activities; the Sect has an impenetrable network of power and retribution and punishes mercilessly those who interfere with its activities, betray it, or refuse to cooperate. Vidal supports this assertion with a series of exemplary tales, including an exhaustive interpretation of Sabato's *The Tunnel*, which includes a blind man, the husband of the victim. The interpretation is a delightful exegesis, and Sabato must have indulged himself out of weariness with the overly serious and clinical interpretations to which his first novel has been subjected.

Finally, the reader is presented with the conviction that he, Vidal, became a target for retribution because of his attempts to confirm his theories about the Sect. The Memorandum, carefully safeguarded in an apartment where it escapes the fire that destroys its author in fulfillment of its prophecy, is designed to serve as a warning to the world of the power and the far-reaching influence of the Sect. The latter part of the document shifts in tone from the sardonic to the surrealistic, and Vidal claims to be under the influence of an agent of the Sect who is about to execute him. The reader realizes, however, that this portion of the document reflects the final disintegration of the man's personality under the weight of its own inner dragons. Realization also comes that the She who appears with ever greater insistence and terror is no blind executioner but in fact Alejandra. Although he has seduced and destroyed her with his own infernal evil, a sense of guilt converts her in his eyes into the agent of his own expiation by fire of the sins of his degenerate soul. For reasons unknown, Vidal is a haunted and tortured man. Somehow he has communicated this burden as a spiritual inheritance to his daughter; by some accord that we, like Martín, are not privileged to comprehend, they go to meet their destiny in the fiery holocaust of the decaying family mansion. The factor that largely justifies taking the Memorandum as a psychoanalytically valid document is the conversion of the elaborate hypotheses concerning the Sect of the Blind and its inescapable revenge into a revelation of the terrifying burden of guilt that has been accumulated in this one man's soul and his subsequent, totally non-Christian drive to purge himself of it.

The bulk of the summary given up to this point, which emphasizes the revelation of Fernando Vidal's inner dragons, has been virtually the only interest of the few previous attempts to come to grips with Sabato's novel. Yet we must find a broader significance for this Memorandum if we are to understand how it relates to Martín's story, purportedly the focus of the novel. It is not enough merely to say that Vidal's memoir uncovers the debauched soul of the man who is responsible for Alejandra's suffering and the anguish it causes Martín in his inability to rationalize the events in which he is ensnared. Such a characterization provides some tie-in with the first two chapters, but it does not justify the length of Vidal's papers.

An initial approximation lies in the superficial significance of Vidal's name, the etymon of which is the Latin *videre*, "to see," to which has been added an adjectival suffix. Thus, he is the seeing one, the seer in both the senses of one who scrutinizes analytically what he perceives around him as well as of one who is able to project his insight onto the level of vatic prophecy. Obviously, this "seeing" stands in metaphoric contrast to the physical sightlessness of the Sect of the Blind, which he pursues and, in his own sick mind, is eventually pursued by. But what Vidal "sees" is not the literal shape of the world—this sight is available to anyone with eyes. His perception is the inner meaning of the universe, and it is a seeing that becomes both an interpretation of his own experience and an urgent warning to all nonblind mankind. One could compound the conceit of seeing, blind, seer, etc.; the basic interrelationship should be apparent enough to obviate an insistence on a detail that is only the exterior patina of the Memorandum's complex fantasy.

Leaving aside the psychoanalytic validity of the document vis-à-vis Vidal's incestuous relationship with Alejandra, one turns to the far more significant factor, the man's scribblings and their meaning in terms of the novel's anti-intellectual and antirational attitudes toward the interpretation of vital, human experience. Consider the ironic implications of the following passages from Vidal's notes:

This Memorandum is intended, after my imminent death, for an institute that believes it worth continuing the investigation of this world that has remained unexplored until today. As such, it is limited to the FACTS as these have happened to me. The value that it possesses, in my judgement, is its absolute objectivity. I want to speak of my experience as an explorer is able to speak of his expedition to the Amazon or to Central Africa. And although, as is only natural, emotion and malice may often confuse me, at least my desire is to be exact and not to allow myself to be swept away by these feelings. I have had frightening experiences, but it is precisely because of them that I want to stick to the facts, even though these facts may cast an unfavorable light on my own life. After what I have said no one in his right mind can claim that the purpose of these papers is to evoke sympathy for my own person.[7]

7. Pt. III, Ch. VI. The first three chapters of this part of the novel were translated by Stuart M. Gross and published as "Report on the Blind . . .," *TriQuarterly*, 13/14 (1968–1969), 95–105.

I'll describe the episode in case you haven't heard it. This painter, Víctor Brauner, had an obsession about blindness and in several of his paintings he did portraits of men with one eye pierced or hanging out, including a self-portrait in which one of his own eyes was missing. Then, right before the war, in an orgy in the study of a member of the surrealist group, a certain Domínguez got drunk and threw a glass at someone. The latter stepped aside, and the glass struck Víctor Brauner, putting one of his eyes out.

So you can see now whether or not we should talk about chance, whether or not chance has any meaning at all among men. On the contrary, men go about like sleepwalkers, moving toward ends which often they can only intuit darkly, but toward which they are attracted like moths to a flame. Thus, Brauner went toward the glass thrown by Domínguez, toward his own blindness. . . .

Note for those who are ingenuous:

THERE ARE NO ACCIDENTS!

And above all, a note for those who after me may read this Memorandum and decide to undertake the search and to go a little further than I did. Such unfortunate precursors like Maupassant (who paid with his madness), Rimbaud (who, despite his flight to Africa, also ended up mad and with gangrene), and so many other anonymous heroes we don't know about who must have ended their days, without anyone knowing about it, between the walls of some madhouse, tortured by political police, asphyxiated in blind wells, swallowed up by a swamp, eaten alive by ants in Africa, devoured by sharks, castrated and sold to Oriental sultans, or, like myself, destined to death by fire.[8]

Of particular significance is the second of these two excerpts for, as in so many parts of the Memorandum, it advances a "proof" of what is being said about the blind via an exemplary and chilling tale. From an extrinsic point of view, one can say that, in passing, much of the Memorandum must have been written by Sabato with a separate novel in mind, so autonomous is the life of development followed by Vidal in the proof of his theories. Yet, within the over-all whole of *On Heroes and Tombs*, of which it

8. Pt. III, Ch. XXXI.

has become a supposedly integral part, Vidal's rantings take on a highly significant function.

Vidal's Memorandum, then, functions as an extended novelistic conceit for the search by the sensitive, intelligent individual after the meaning of human destiny. Beneath the surface of the Judeo–Christian unity of Western civilization there have existed many such elaborate, usually apocalyptic, explanations of the cosmos. Many, like that of the Rosicrucians for example, have been of particular appeal to men like Fernando Vidal, gifted with exceptional intellect but possessed by emotional restlessness. As far as the novel is concerned, Vidal's illumination is a private one, destined for communication to the rest of mankind only after his sacrifice. Indeed, Vidal, in his role as prophetic seer and indefatigable pursuer of the secrets of the Sect, must have come to see himself as a sacrificial figure, as a Christ: Through the contributions of his investigations and the sacrifice that he has accepted with resignation will mankind be made aware of the truths that have remained hidden until now. His closing sentences read like a martyr's farewell, as he faces with calm the denouement of the role he has assumed:

I also know that my time is limited and that my death awaits me. And what is strange and for me incomprehensible is that that death awaits me in some way through my own will, because no one will come for me here. I will be the one to go, the one who must go, to where the prophecy is to be fulfilled.

Cunning, the desire to live, despair, all have made me imagine a thousand flights, a thousand forms to escape fate. But how can anyone escape his own fate?

Therefore, I'll close my Memorandum here, which I'm going to safeguard in a place where the Sect can't find it.

It's twelve o'clock midnight. I'm on my way there.

I know that she'll be waiting for me.[9]

Vidal's calm in the face of his impending fiery end for sins committed against the Sect derives from his satisfaction with the validity of his discoveries. No matter that the discoveries may in fact be the inventions, the fan-

9. Pt. III, Ch. XXXVIII.

tasies of a madman; his end is at once a confession, an
exculpation, and the presentiment of a symbolic retribution for his cruelty and debauchery. In terms of what the
reader has come to know about Alejandra and about the
individuals affected always for the worse by the self-styled
Nietzschean man that was Fernando Vidal, it becomes
less incredible to see the "Memorandum on the Blind" as
the product of a superior but definitely psychotically
alienated mind that justifies its author's existence and beliefs not only to the outside world but to himself as well.

Vidal's memoir is undoubtedly the most captivating
segment of the work, and, while it has not attracted major
critical commentary, it has rightly been recognized as perhaps the most creative of Sabato's efforts. All of which, to
be sure, is highly ironic. For, if the Memorandum possesses the two levels of meaning described—one vis-à-vis Vidal's soul and one vis-à-vis man's compulsion to construct
an all-encompassing interpretation of experience—that it
should be the most memorable contribution of Sabato's
novel underlines ironically the very point that he appears
to be making in incorporating it within the over-all pattern of *On Heroes and Tombs.*

Part Four of the novel, "An Unknown God," details on
three levels the repercussions of the expiatory conflagra-
tion of Alejandra and Fernando. There are also periodic
flashbacks to the final absurdity, as seen by Lieutenant
Olmos, of Lavalle's fateful March to the North. On one
level we have Martín's despair, his nightmarish journey
through nocturnal Buenos Aires, and his liberating decision, as a result of the words of the humble prostitute,
to set out for the South with the truck driver Bucich. The
trajectory of Martín's despair demonstrates once again,
after the engrossing interlude of Vidal's communiqué to
mankind, the boy's utter inability to comprehend the
events that swirl around him. The opening paragraph,
which records Martín's premonition in a nightmare of
Alejandra's symbolic death by fire, stresses how his grasp
of the mystery of the girl remains for him forever locked in
a chamber of the primitive subconscious:

On the night of June 24, 1956 [*sic*, for 1955], Martín was unable to sleep. He kept seeing Alejandra again as on that first time in the park when she approached him. Then, chaotically, moments both tender and terrible would come to mind. And that first encounter, unknown and marvelous. Until little by little a heavy drowsiness overtook him and his imagination began to unfold in that realm of ambiguity. Then he thought he heard distant and melancholy bells and an uncertain moan, perhaps an indecipherable call. Slowly it became a disconsolate and barely perceptible voice that repeated his name over and over, while the bells tolled with ever greater intensity until finally they were ringing with true fury. The sky, that dream sky, now seemed illuminated by the bloody splendor of a fire. And then he saw Alejandra advancing toward him in the reddened shadows, with her face contorted and her arms outstretched, moving her lips as if distressed and silently repeating that call. "*Alejandra!*" Martín shouted, waking up. When he turned on the light, shaking, he saw that he was all alone in the room.[10]

From here on, until the resolute decision that finally breaks the girl's spell over him, life for Martín is a living, waking nightmare. He is able to find some alleviation throughout the affair with Alejandra by expressing his frustrating lack of comprehension to his ever-attentive but uncommunicative friend Bruno, although it seems that for significant reasons Bruno is unavailable as a silent witness to the youth's final agony of confusion (Pt. IV, Ch. II):

For days he hung around the house, waiting for them to end the guard that had been posted. He limited himself to looking from afar at what remained of that room in which he had known ecstasy and despair: a skeleton blackened by the flames which the spiral staircase seemed to be trying to reach like a twisted and pathetic gesture. And when night fell, on walls poorly illuminated by the light on the corner, he could see the openings of the doors and the window like hollow sockets of a bleached skull.

What was he seeking, why did he want to get in? He could not have replied himself. But patiently he waited for the use-

10. Pt. IV, Ch. I.

less guard to be withdrawn, and then that same night he climbed the fence and went in. With a flashlight he traveled the same path that a millennium before he had followed with her for the first time on that summer night. He went along the edge of the house and walked toward the belvedere. . . .

The night was cold and cloudy, the silence of the morning was profound. The far-off echo of a ship's horn could be heard, and then again the nothingness. For a while Martín remained still but upset. Then (but it could only have been the result of his tensed imagination) he heard the weak but clear voice of Alejandra saying only "Martín." The boy, overcome, leaned his body against the wall and stayed that way for a long, long time.[11]

Novelistic Unity

Bruno, the mute analyst, the omnipresent confessor, emerges in Chapter III of Part Four as a member of the drama of the Vidal Olmos family. Once a close friend of Alejandra's mother, Bruno at this point serves to corroborate our sense of the stigma of tragedy borne by that family from the time of Lavalle's march and to deepen our perception of the pursuit after the "hidden truth" by those affected by Alejandra and Fernando's strange relationship. In earlier segments of the novel (throughout Parts One and Two), Martín's story is communicated to the reader through Bruno's recollection of the youth's terrible outpourings of anguish. But Bruno's own position as the perceiver of Martín's role and also as a revealing confidant of Vidal's is communicated via an unidentified narrator, presumably Sabato. The new narrator enters at this point to stand in a position related toward Bruno's recollection of his youth with Fernando that corresponds to Martín's outpourings concerning his own relationship, a generation later, with Alejandra and, unknowingly but through her, with the hidden father. Thus, Bruno and Martín are drawn together, fused functionally and structurally, in this coda to the tragedy of the Olmos family. Both are ultimately involved in versions of the

11. Pt. IV, Ch. IV.

same quest, that of an understanding, a key, to the mean-ing of the recent events. Along another axis, the reader becomes aware that a century earlier, a forebear of the Olmos family, during a critical period in the history of the then new Argentine nation, had also been involved in an identical attempt to come to grips with a reality that he sensed was dissolving into nightmare around him. Olmos's puzzlement at the chaos of the once-glorious resis-tance to Rosas in turn prefigures the efforts of his descen-dant, Fernando Vidal Olmos, to bring the world of his experience into a focus of understanding:

> *Not even two-hundred men remain, and now they are no longer even soldiers: they are beings, defeated and dirty, and many of them no longer know why they are fighting. Lieu-tenant Celedonio Olmos, like the rest, rides grim and silent, remembering his father, Captain Olmos, and his brother, both killed in Quebracho Herrado.*
>
> *Eight-hundred leagues of defeats. He no longer under-stands anything, and the malign words of Iriarte constantly come back to him: the mad general [Lavalle], the man who did not know what he wanted. And hadn't Solana Sotomayor left Brizuela for Lavalle? He can see Brizuela now: unkempt, drunk, surrounded by dogs. Let none of Lavalle's messengers get near! And now isn't that girl from Salta there at his side? He no longer understands a thing. And everything was so clear two years ago: Liberty or Death. But now. . . .*
>
> *The world has become a chaos. And he thinks about his mother and his childhood. But the figure of Brigadier Bri-zuela comes back to him: a dirty vociferating rag doll. The mastiffs surround him, frothing at the mouth. And then he tries again to recall that childhood.*[12]

Thus, on several simultaneous levels throughout the novel at least four individuals (five, if we include the shadowy consciousness of Alejandra; six, if we count the anonymous narrator whose narrative we also assume to be an attempt at comprehension) seek the meaning of an apparent reality that forever eludes them. In one sense, the reader, who is often several times removed from the

12. Pt. IV, Ch. V.

narrative (for example, the reader is told what Bruno tells him that Martín reported to him what Alejandra revealed in one of her outbursts), enjoys the privileged position of being able to compare the overlapping—if not entirely complementary—stories of the principal characters. To this extent, Martín, the central consciousness of the novel, and the reader stand in structural juxtaposition to each other. The novelist needs such a juxtaposition in order to reinforce his concept of novelistic *non*omniscience. Although on one level the reader enjoys a point of view superior to Martín's (he is permitted to see the Memorandum and to hear Bruno's story, both of which are inaccessible to the youth), in the end only the naive reader will believe that he has acquired a more solid understanding of events than Martín. The reader, too, becomes involved in the quest for the truth, for the key. Yet, five hundred pages later, he still has been given only a greater number of pieces to the puzzle and little or no instruction in how to fit them together.

The "Rashomon syndrome," of which Sabato makes use, must therefore be labeled ironic. In Akutagawa's novelette, the reader is presented with five points of view explaining the death of a man. One realizes that the truth is not unitary but multiple, and it emerges only with the addition of that unknown member of the equation, man himself. In Sabato's novel, while we are privileged to have a number of points of view that ostensibly contribute to our knowledge of the warped Olmos family, the perceptive reader must admit that he has been given insufficient information in order to arrive at the full truth of the events in the novel and their motivation. In part, we can say that this "informational failure" of the novel derives from the nature of the human consciousnesses that provide the reader with perspectives on the mystery. It is a truism that every man remembers the facts of his existence in terms both of what he is and what he wants to be. But beyond the inevitable failures of the individual, all-too-human reporter, we have Sabato's clear intent that the reader cannot satisfy his desire for facile and exhaustive answers. It is a "clear intent" only because the critic must assume that a novel's structure results from a well-conceived authorial plan and is not a lamentable mistake. To this extent, the release and relative spiritual tranquility achieved by Martín when he finally abandons his pointless quest for truth can be interpreted only as symbolic of man's overly intellectualized approach to the eternal questions whirling about in his feverish mind. The result can only be the lunacy and self-destruction of a Fernando Vidal.

Within the context of these comments, it is useful to consider Vidal, Bruno, and Martín as degrees of the same phenomenon—that is, the quest for the truth of human experience. Vidal, in his acute derangement, believes that he has found it, and his Memorandum is simply a novel, a creative exercise in which the truth is given fanciful and exemplary representation.

Bruno, the self-proclaimed literatus of the novel, has been engaged for years in attempting to unravel the complex fabric of Vidal and the people under his power, although the reader is not made aware of this private quest until near the end of the novel.[13] Throughout these pages Bruno reveals himself through his emotional inadequacies and through his personal failure to fabricate a novelistically coherent pattern of meaning out of thirty years of wrestling with the knowledge of events:

> Thus I too [like Martín with Alejandra] was unable to learn anything about what went on in that most secret, and for me most sought after, part of Georgina's soul.
> Why, my God, why?[14]

Martín, as I have stressed repeatedly, is able to experience recent events only through a deep emotional

13. Pt. IV, Ch. III: "Now, thirty years later, I'm still trying to comprehend the precise relationship between those two [Fernando and his cousin Georgina, Alejandra's mother—also an incestuous relationship], and I find it impossible to do so."
14. Pt. IV, Ch. III.

involvement with Alejandra that contrasts with the clinically detached attitude assumed by Bruno after the passage of many years. Indeed, it is in view of this relative detachment alone that we can explain his failure to confide in Martín his own revealing involvement with that tragic family. Where Bruno's role is, after so many years of involvement, essentially the active one of the novelist manqué who can never quite successfully orchestrate his material, Martín's position is that of passive emotion, deeply felt and profoundly marked by the uncontrollable events that swirl around him. In one of Bruno's few comments on Martín to come to the reader's attention, he prophesies that, despite the boy's ability to overcome his initial suicidal shock through the healthy release of the journey South, he will carry subconsciously throughout his life the burden of his brief contact with Alejandra:

> Bruno learned about the greater part of those decisive facts only after Martín had returned from that remote region where he had gone to bury himself, only after time seemed to have settled that pain in the depths of his soul, a pain which seemed to return to disturb his spirit with the agitation and the movement which accompanied his new encounter with the people and objects that were indissolubly connected with the tragedy. And although by that time Alejandra's body had rotted and turned to dust, that boy, who was now truly a man, continued nevertheless to be obsessed by his love. And who knows for how many years, and likely up until the day of his death, he would continue to be obsessed. All of which, as far as Bruno was concerned, constituted something like a proof of the immortality of the soul.[15]

Vidal and Bruno are somewhat sinister and unsympathetic as far as the reader is concerned, wrapped in the egotism of their basically intellectual quest, but Martín emerges as Everyman in his grief, his confusion, his impotence. At the same time, the flexibility of his personality, his ability to rise above self-pity over his bleak childhood and to make an honest effort to bring a relationship

15. Pt. IV, Ch. II.

to Alejandra and to rescue her from the inner dragon, and later his success in achieving some peace with himself after the final act of her tragedy—these are all aspects that reinforce Martín's strength as a symbol of modern man and his burdens. On the immediate level of a page-by-page examination of the work, one realizes the extent to which, despite his innate limitations, the youth is the only truly sympathetic figure of the work. The author predisposes us toward Martín while repelling us from Bruno, the emotionally inadequate parasite of the tragedy of the Olmos line. At the same time, neither Vidal nor Alejandra are designed to evoke the reader's empathy, Vidal because of the obvious psychotic cruelty of his personality, and Alejandra, although we come to sense the deep agony of her soul, because of the extent of her alienation when we first meet her. In the end, only Martín and the pasteboard "good folk" of the lower class are capable of engaging suitable identification with the supposedly normal, healthy emotions of the audience.

Martín is central in another, more strictly novelistic sense, for it is he who ties together the two historical levels of the novel. Although one's initial impulse might be to link Lieutenant Olmos with his descendant Vidal in their common sense of the ridiculous chaos of human events, the essential confusion of Lieutenant Olmos contrasts with the paranoid self-assurance of Vidal. Moreover, the italicized segments concerning the March to the North are always presented in conjunction with passages that involve Martín and thus suggest a closer tie between these two youths, separated by almost exactly one hundred years of national history and national disaster. Thus, we have Lieutenant Olmos, the waning dictatorship of Juan Manuel Rosas, the March to the North, and the defense by the tenuous community of intellectuals against the barbarity of Rosas's national government vs Martín, the waning dictatorship of Juan Domingo Perón, Martín's personal march to the South, and the implicit defense, through the structure of the novel, of the inherent hu-

manitarian and fraternal values of the lumpen proletariat. In this respect, *On Heroes and Tombs* possesses a
built-in irony that is especially noticeable to the Argentine reader. Published at a time when Argentina was still
struggling to overcome the legacy of Perón's dictatorship,
the novel produces a certain local impact in its revision-
ary portrayal of the classes that supported Perón, particularly in the alliance between them and the middle-class
would-be writer.

Nevertheless, this is only a purely local detail of the
novel that adds to it a new dimension for the reader familiar with Argentine history. It does not lessen in any
way the more general anti-intellectual trajectory of the
narrative as a whole. There will always be details in the
background references of foreign fiction that are beyond
the grasp of all but the most knowledgeable of readers,
but which are comprehensible within the immediate context in which they are presented. For example, one need
not be familiar with the political and social events leading
up to the burning of the churches the night of Alejandra's
death: That it is a national immolation related to the
purgative death by fire of the last of a famous family is
clear and forceful enough within the context of the narrative. Yet a deeper understanding unquestionably results
from apprehending the connections between the holy
statues that Martín helps to save and the warped female
principle invoked by Alejandra through her father's fantastic visions (the feud between the Church and Perón
that resulted in the burnings stemmed in part from the
Church's refusal to replace the images of the Virgin with
those of the masses' new Holy Mother, Eva Perón).

The lengthy and complex structure of the novel permits quite an elaborate schematic representation for Martín's position as the controlling, structurally central
consciousness of *On Heroes and Tombs*. It supports the
details of the preceding characterization of the twisted
relationships between the various individuals of the
novel.

On the level of artistic or narrative perception, we have

seen a gradated relationship between Martín, the confused, would-be artist seeker; Bruno, the middle-aged
novelist manqué; and the unidentified narrator (the
equally, ostensibly perplexed author?), ultimately responsible for the novelistic text.

On the personal level that justifies Martín as a sympathetic figure of Everyman, he serves as a counterbalancing
force to Fernando Vidal, the figure of an ultimately triumphant evil. One is tempted to counterpose an Angel of
Darkness, an ironic epithet for Vidal in his explorations
of the Shadowy Realm of the human soul given objective
correlation in the Sect of the Blind, and an Angel of Light,
the innocent youth who readily accepts the challenge
of darkness but who is ultimately defeated by it. Vis-à-vis
Alejandra, these two figures come to constitute the antag-
onistic forces within her soul. As the result of years of
association and influence, as though she were the subject
of some hideous experiment in perdition by a spiritual
heir to the Marquis de Sade, Alejandra has come completely under the spell of her father. One should not mistake her homicide-suicide as willful revenge against the
man, for, as he himself reveals, she is merely an instru-
ment in the self-destruction that he has accepted as his
destiny. Alejandra has been carefully conditioned to exercise a ritual role in her father's designs, and her final
incendiary act, based on purgation by fire, is the culmina-
tion of a finely developed guilt.

On the other side is Martín, who attempts to "save"
Alejandra from the terrible "dragon" that he senses lies
within her. But the "princess" has already been too thoroughly consumed from within to be rescued by the timid,
ineffectual love of the boy. We soon realize that their
"chance" meeting in Lezama Park, which was frequented
by Martín in his adolescent self-pity, was carefully ar-
ranged by Alejandra as a last appeal to the outside world.
But Alejandra has remained sufficiently lucid to realize
that her sickness is beyond remedy, or at least beyond the
powers of Martín, and she warns him with words he cannot understand that it is better for him not to seek her
out:

"Yes, Alejandra, of course I feel sorry for you. Can't I see, after all, how horribly you're suffering? I don't want you to suffer. I swear that this won't happen again."

Little by little she calmed down. Finally she wiped her tears away with a handkerchief.

"No, Martín," she said. "It's better that we don't see each other any more. Because sooner or later we would have to part under even worse circumstances. There are hideous things inside me that I'm unable to overcome."[16]

This scene is repeated in variations throughout the latter half of Part Two, until it becomes a rhythmic pattern of Alejandra's suffering, Martín's love but inability to understand, her sending him away to protect *him*, and her agreement to see him once more because of his devotion. The pattern not only reveals a humane side of this truly tragic woman but also emphasizes the humble, common decency of the boy. Although certainly not a motif of the novel, their sexual relationship becomes an explicit correlative of their total relationship. Although sex is repulsive to Alejandra, in whom it undoubtedly evokes fearsome memories of her father, she accedes to Martín's puppy-dog approach as the supreme submission to his devotion, only to submit herself afterwards to a purgative cleansing of truly biblical proportions. Indeed, her acts of purification, which follow fits of apparent epilepsy like mystic transports, suggest an interpretation of these seizures as domination by some infernal sexuality (see the confusion of epilepsy and sex in Chapters XVII and XVIII of Part I).

I have mentioned Martin's function as a central, focusing consciousness on the sociopolitical level, and these observations need not be repeated here. It might be added however that, within their respective historical milieus, both Olmos and Martín live through momentous historical moments. For Martín, the moment is correlated with a personal story of various national overtones concerning Olmos's descendants. Both are in a certain sense the men of their respective historical futures. Certainly, the likes

16. Pt. II, Ch. XXI.

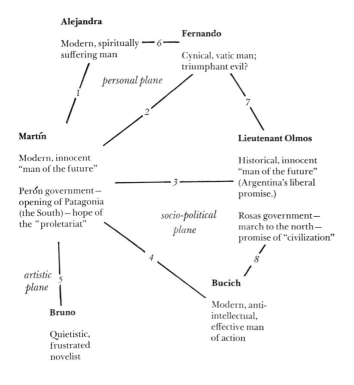

Functional Relationships

1. "Salvation" through normal sense of preservation, ineffectual but healthy love, attraction to the emotionally mysterious.

2. Synchronic social and spiritual antithesis.

3. Diachronic social antithesis but spiritual affinity.

4. Synchronic social (both "nobodies") and spiritual affinity on a normal, manly, and fraternal level (cf. 1).

5. Narrative relationship, levels of telling.

6. Perdition, psychotic destruction through effectual but unhealthy love (incest).

7. Diachronic social affinity (both aristocrats) but spiritual antithesis.

8. Undeveloped but implied diachronic social and spiritual antithesis.

of Olmos made the old Argentina, and the implication is
that, with the fall of the Perón regime, which supposedly
ended the old rule of the oligarchs, the Martíns and the
Buciches will build the new Argentina. It is in the nature
of such prophetic fiction—and it is this aspect of the novel
that I find most unsatisfactory even though I am able to
appreciate its interrelationships with the rest of the
work—that fate give the lie to such visions. The significance of the journey south remains fanciful prophecy, at
least for the moment and for the foreseeable future.

It is only within this framework that we can grasp
Sabato's work, not just as a novel (one function, as we
have seen, of its inner metanovelistic structure is to reject
the novel as a statement of truth), not as a document (despite the documentary illusion of Vidal's report and the
various levels of narrative reporting), but as the patterned
pseudomyth. A sense of the unexplainable whole is communicated to the sympathetic reader, who must create
from it his own understanding of this exceedingly perplexing but unmistakably masterful piece of fiction.
Myth is an easy word to use; surely it is one of the most
worn words of criticism, and tacking *pseudo* onto it does
little to make it more meaningful. Yet, there can be no
question that there is a fundamental irony underlying
Sabato's novel, an irony that hinges both on his communication to us of the inability of man to construct an adequate explanation of his ambiguous and confusing
experience and his, the novelist's, projection in his novel
of an alternative version of Argentina as a correlation of
that explanatory failure. The novel posits its immediate
point of departure on a series of public and private events,
events that are inextricably related to each other and,
as I have shown, that a series of actors in those events
attempt in vain to explain, to fit into a coherent and all-
encompassing order. On the highest levels—those in the
novel and in the mind of the reader of the novel—the
sardonic implication is clear: Both novelist and reader
will be in the end unsuccessful in imposing an explanation on the events described in the novel (a statement

which has as its corollary the assertion that any perceived order is illusory—the unquestionable conclusion to be drawn from Vidal's deadly serious but wildly far-fetched Memorandum). In Martín's troubled thoughts, Lieutenant Olmos's diary, Vidal's Memorandum, Bruno's incessant interrogations, and, ultimately, Sabato's novel are ironic *attempts* to construct a myth, a transcendental explanation that will account magically and effectively for the events and the experiences that befall man.

Both Vidal and the novelist succeed in constructing apparently coherent explanations, the Memorandum and the novel. But the explanations are only apparent, and the far-fetchedness of Vidal's writings and the multiple ambiguities of the novel that encapsulate the writings are ironic testimony to the inevitable failings of any attempt at an explanation. This is why Martín is the *beatus ille*, for his salvation clearly lies in the new life he has chosen, released from the haunting spell of Alejandra, and the demand, which in a sense she unconsciously placed upon him, to know and to understand the incomprehensible. Sabato's novel is an alternate version, in the sense that it contrasts hypotheses concerning the nature of Argentine society and its history and that it manipulates a series of character oppositions toward suggesting various explanations of that society and history and of the public and private experiences the Argentine has been called upon to live. But while Sabato's novel is complete in the same sense that Vidal's Memorandum is complete, his pseudomyth is in the end just that—pseudo, a nonexplanation, a pattern of events and relationships that do not coalesce into an ultimate explanation of Argentine "heroes and tombs." The reader is left with a brilliant sketch of the possible beginnings of an explanation, of an inventory of the pieces that any putative totalizing vision must account for, and an ironic superstructure which is conclusive in its rejection of a final explanation for those fascinating and deeply troubling pieces.

JULIO CORTÁZAR'S rise in Latin-American letters has been nothing less than meteoric. He was born in Brussels in 1914 of Argentine parents and has been a publishing author of prose fiction since the appearance of his first two works (a collection of poems and a drama) in the late forties. Despite this literary product, Cortázar is not included in the Argentine volumes of the Pan-American Union's *Diccionario de la literatura latinoamericana* (1960–1961). On the other hand, during the past few years, following the enthusiastic reception of his works by literary critics on both sides of the Atlantic, at least ten books on Cortázar have appeared and a bibliography of learned and popular articles that already challenges in number the listings for such venerable figures as José Hernández, Ricardo Güiraldes, and Jorge Luis Borges.

Almost all of Cortázar's works have been well received, although some of his recent attempts at mixed-media writing tempt accusations of commercialism. Three of his four novels are available in well-reviewed English translations: *Los premios* (*The Prizewinners* [1960]), *Rayuela* (*Hopscotch* [1963]), and *62: modelo para armar* (*62: A Model Kit* [1968]). It is probable that the fourth, *El libro de Manuel* (1973), will also be translated soon into English. The first two are considered major works. Five collections of short stories and short fiction published between 1951 and 1966 have served to solidify his fame in that form. One short story, "Las babas del diablo" ("The Devil's Slobber"), from the 1959 collection *Las armas secretas* (*Secret Weapons*), was the basis of Michelangelo Antonioni's 1967 film, *Blow-Up*.

Cortázar, who has resided in the Europe of his birth and is now a French citizen (he works as a translator for UNESCO in Paris) strikes many Latin Americans as somewhat out of touch with an Argentina which he has only briefly called home. In this sense, he is a prime Argentine example of the contemporary Latin-American man of letters who, absent from his homeland for political and personal reasons and identifying with Europe, resembles the Lost Generation of American writers. Indeed, Cortázar is easily faulted for his occasionally outmoded Argentine slang and his Frenchified pronunciation of Spanish. Yet, a central importance of his novel *Hopscotch* is the close, sardonic scrutiny of ties to Paris of the New-World intellectual and artist. Perhaps the brilliance of this scrutiny, which becomes a totalizing vision of man's spiritual quest, is the factor that most solidly ensures Cortázar's importance as a member of the current international set of Latin-American writers as well as his importance as their most distinguished and unsentimental commentator.

*I jes hope what I been writing down hear do somebody some good
so he take a good look at how he livin and he dont be sorry when
it too late and everythin is gone down the draine cause it his own
fault.*
CÉSAR BRUTO, *what I Would Like to
Be If I Wasn't What I Am*
(Chapter: "A St. Bernard Dog").[1]

Sabato's *Gesamtkunstwerk* may be the first major work
in Argentine fiction to free itself radically from the
stream-of-consciousness narrative and to move toward an
audaciously formless or nonlinear epicomythic narrative.
But thanks to immediate translation into several lan-
guages, including English, Julio Cortázar's *Hopscotch*
(*Rayuela*) has dominated Argentine literature since its
original publication in 1963. Along with perhaps a half-
dozen other titles, *Hopscotch* has been a dominant force
in Latin-American fiction, both from the point of view of
the Latin-American writers and from the enthusiastic perspective of American and continental readers. Yet, despite
the importance of both Sabato and Cortázar in the re-
visionary vanguard of Argentine fiction, it is only to
Cortázar one points when speaking of the "international-
ism" attained by Gabriel García Márquez, Mario Vargas
Llosa, Carlos Fuentes, Guillermo Cabrera Infante.

These writers, along with perhaps a dozen more, constitute the vital force of a Latin-American fiction that has
received widespread international attention never before
accorded Spanish-American writers. They have produced
a homogeneity of outlook and practice that transcends

1. Second prefatory quotation to *Hopscotch*; translated from
the Spanish by Gregory Rabassa (New York: Pantheon Books,
1966). All excerpts are from this edition, based on the original edition in Spanish, *Rayuela* (Buenos Aires: Editorial Sudamericana,
1963).

national boundaries in a way reminiscent of turn-of-the-century Modernism. *Hopscotch* lacks the dynamic spectacle that dominates Sabato's novel and *On Heroes and Tombs*; it tends toward an asceptic diffuseness that threatens, like experience itself, to vanish into nothingness.

Despite *Hopscotch*'s obvious excellence, one never ceases to be amazed at the critical bibliography it has fostered, the ultimate academic tribute to a definitive work. Part of this critical reception goes beyond a merely repetitive adulation. A great deal of ink has been invested in orienting both the amateur and the professional reader in "playing the game" demanded by the six hundred pages of *Hopscotch*. Not since Joyce's *Finnegan's Wake* has the reader been so utterly at a loss as to how to proceed in the task of interpretation. Kurt Vonnegut's work is the only parallel example in American fiction that comes in mind; both he and Cortázar have burdened the harried reader with extraordinary interpretive demands, which are so characteristic of innovative art.[2] It is not so much the rather extreme accusation that these writers have destroyed the traditional novel (whatever it was) and have substituted in its place the "non-novel" of man's contemporary anticulture. Rather, it is a matter of acknowl-

2. Much has been said concerning the demands placed upon the reader and the supposed significance of these demands in "molding" a more involved, self-conscious reader. See, for example, the essay by Mario Benedetti, "Julio Cortázar, un narrador para los lectores cómplices," *Tiempo moderno*, 1, ii (1964), 16–19, as well as comments in the monographs listed in the Bibliography. Cortázar's own words within the novel on the many occasions when the nature of fiction is raised should also be noted (Chs. 109, 112, 115, 116, 141, 145, 154, among others). Much of this comment is clearly the inflated rhetoric of what is spectacularly "new." Certainly, all great works of literature have demanded an active participation on the part of the reader, if no more than to resolve the ambiguities of life transmitted via the ambiguities of narrative structure. But, then, this is not the place to scorn the claims of both the critics and the novel. To a great extent the critics have certainly been influenced by the explicitness of the novel, and it serves an unmistakably novelistic end within the work. For the English reader, the best presentation of these claims remains Luis Harss and Barbara Dohmann, *Into the Mainstream*, Ch. VI, "Julio Cortázar, or the Slap in the Face."

edging those factors that are innovative in their works: a particular nonlinear and nonautonomous concept of human personality and the themes, techniques, and structure that this notion may imply. Adapting the task of criticism to account adequately for these innovations without claiming the dubious presence of an antiliterature, one ought to be able to achieve a coherent appreciation of the impact of such works as *Hopscotch*.

Where does one begin the study of such a protean novel? Despite its length, *Hopscotch* is the story of one insignificant man's frustrating attempt to convince himself of the existential validity of Western culture, typified by the mystique of Paris, and to fill the void of his existence with a pattern of some transcendent meaning through various "games" undertaken in Buenos Aires. It is pompous and trivial to say that the main character, Horacio Oliveira, is the lost and bewildered figure of modern Everyman that has assumed innumerable pseudonyms in the Western novel of the last few decades. To a certain extent, Oliveira must be such an Everyman. A common denominator of the contemporary novelistic vanguard is the rejection of individual human autonomy, at least on the level of significant experience, and the substitution of the mythic prototype. For half of the novel, Oliveira is an Argentine exile in seamy Left-Bank Paris. But his spiritual crises are less Latin-American than they are "existentially primitive." His greatest interest as a novelistic creation lies in the implicit rejection of the typical Western anguish which impels him in his games of identity.

A casual reading of the novel may impress one as so much absurd nothingness, and a closer examination only substantiates this assessment of Oliveira's role. But the milieu that constitutes the traditional measure of the middle-aged Sartrean generation (it has been some years since Oliveira was a romantic youth) is equally absurd: Paris, the Left Bank, commitment, phatic orgies of pseudo-philosophy, cigarettes of dubious content, cheap booze, and scratchy records—in short, the whole arty pose of the alienated. Oliveira plays his chosen part to perfection, but the script has become dreadfully worn and no one is listening closely any more. When Oliveira returns to Buenos Aires at the close of the first part of the novel, his mental ramblings on the game of hopscotch reveal a subconscious awareness of the futility of his favorite games:

Hopscotch is played with a pebble that you move with the tip of your toe. The things you need: a sidewalk, a pebble, a toe, and a pretty chalk drawing, preferably in colors. On top is Heaven, on the bottom is Earth, it's very hard to get the pebble up to Heaven, you almost always miscalculate and the stone goes off the drawing. But little by little you start to get the knack of how to jump over the different squares (spiral hopscotch, rectangular hopscotch, fantasy hopscotch, not played very often) and then one day you learn how to leave Earth and make the pebble climb up into Heaven (Et tous nos amours, Emmanuele was sobbing face down), the worst part of it is that precisely at that moment, when practically no one has learned how to make the pebble climb up into Heaven, childhood is over all of a sudden and you're into novels, into the anguish of the senseless divine trajectory, into the speculation about another Heaven that you have to learn to reach too. And since you have come out of childhood (Je n'oublierai pas le temps des cerises, Emmanuele was kicking about on the floor) you forget that in order to get to Heaven you have to have a pebble and a toe.[3]

By the time Oliveira abandons Paris, past the middle of the novel—250 pages of comings and goings—the reader realizes that Oliveira is unable to verbalize his discovery that his exquisite anguish is nothing but the black comedy of a vacuous existentialism: Oliveira has been playing a child's game which he ought to have outgrown long ago. Nothing is more comically pathetic than the middle-aged "stranger," and his persistence in the role only underlines his failure to convince himself that the road to truth which he has chosen is the way to truth. Oliveira's futile hadji to Paris functions on several levels of meaning. This circumstance contributes to establishment of the nonspe-

3. Ch. 36, p. 214.

cificity of his character and the vagueness of his personal identity. *Hopscotch* is not only in great part a spoof of the existential ethos that has become so trite in our nuclear society, but it is also the means to strike some heavy blows against the fawning New-World attachment to Paris, that putative intellectual center of the Western world.

Defying the cultural imperialism of the Alliance Française, Cortázar speaks directly to Argentina's traditional dependence on France as the source of all that is civilized and intellectually meaningful. The dependence is still very much there, much as one finds in turn-of-the-century Mexico or the United States (for example, the novels of Henry James, who was not reluctant to strike a similar sardonic note over the attachment). For the United States of today, France is not a cultural threat, but her dominion over Argentine culture, although waning, persists and Paris remains the Mecca of the Oliveiras who strive to transcend national society to find themselves on a purportedly international level. That Cortázar has been a sort of Oliveira serves to compound the irony. I return to this aspect of *Hopscotch* in subsequent pages. For the moment, no initial characterization of the novel is more appropriate than that of Oliveira as the provincial Argentine, the New-World primitive, who sees Paris as the fount of spiritual wisdom. He ultimately returns to Buenos Aires, the city built in humble tribute to the French capital, to work out there the more mature versions of what had become a sterile and silly tourism.

Hopscotch's unity is the product of the relationship between infantile and mature—or, one might say, eccentrically unique—versions of the eponymic game. The novel comprises three distinct sections: a first part consisting of an essentially linear narrative, in retrospect, of Oliveira's Paris quest; a second part, also more or less linear, that recounts his adventures upon returning to Buenos Aires; and a third part made up of an assortment of jottings, newspaper clippings, extracts from one Morelli's notebooks on how to write a novel, epigrams for the Horacian man, etc. The feature that has attracted some attention for this disposition of the 600 pages and 155 "chapters" of the novel is the set of instructions to the reader:

TABLE OF INSTRUCTIONS

In its own way, this book consists of many books, but two books above all.

The first can be read in a normal fashion and it ends with Chapter 56, at the close of which there are three garish little stars which stand for the words The End. Consequently, the reader may ignore what follows with a clean conscience.

The second should be read by beginning with Chapter 73 and then following the sequence indicated at the end of each chapter. In case of confusion or forgetfulness, one need only consult the following list.[4]

At least superficially, *Hopscotch* is self-consciously direct, and it is not difficult to imagine most readers scrupulously following the plan that will take them through all three parts, only to end up, like the needle stuck in the last groove of a broken record, on the recursive nature of Chapters 58 and 131. Chapters 55, 57, and 59 are not mentioned in the Table of Instructions (Chapters 54, 56, 58, and 60 are included). Chapters 55, 57, and 59 serve to close the novel for those who read only the first two parts consecutively and omit the third section of miscellanea. Noteworthy in this extrinsic organization of the novel are the implications concerning form vs formlessness in both a philosophical as well as an esthetic sense. At issue is the extent to which the universe and its diverse manifestations—from the orbits of the planets down to the playing of a hand of bridge—are subject to ideal patterns of form.

4. Unnumbered table following the title page. Note that two types of numberings are scrambled together. Chapters 1–54, 56, and 58 are given in proper numerical order (all but 58 correspond to the first two "narrative" parts of the novel), while the remaining chapters, from the last part, are interspersed in an apparently random order. The formal structure of the novel is examined in Ana María Barrenechea, "La estructura de *Rayuela*, de Julio Cortázar," in Julio Lafforgue, *Nueva novela latinoamericana*, II, 222–47.

Although anthropological structuralism, a sort of secular Platonism, has arisen in the non-American West to replace it (see the writings of Claude Lévi-Strauss, who is quoted in the "extra" Chapter 59), the viewpoint that we vaguely call Platonism has been so generalized in our culture that it is difficult for us to comprehend the esthetic controversies surrounding the problem of artistic form. What we have is the external formalism of Platonism vs the internal formalism unconsciously assumed by cultural and societal manifestations.

These are the structures to which Lévi-Strauss's investigations are directed, and his influence on literary theory has been enormous. Therefore, when Cortázar begins with such an artificially elaborate scheme, easily replaced with a more conventional blending together of the third part and the two narrative parts, the critic suspects an ironic hoax. *Hopscotch*, surely, cannot pretend to be the *Divine Comedy,* with its intricate mathematical structure intended to mirror the grand scheme of the universe in a humble work of vernacular poetry. Oliveira's anguish stems from an existence to be lived without convincing rules, without transcendental patterns that comfort in their all-encompassing mechanisms. The world of *Hopscotch* is precisely a world in which this comfort is lacking, and to adorn its fictional representation with a spurious pattern is a heavy-handed irony against the reader who follows the directions with passive good faith. Indeed, Cortázar remarks rather cavalierly that his work can be read "any old way," a remark that deserves greater attention than the Table of Instructions.

But there is another way to interpret Cortázar's scheme, and this brings us to the heart of the title's meaning. Let us assume that the game of hopscotch is somehow a persuasive symbol for man's existential pilgrimage as he hops about here and there on one foot trying to get from Earth to Heaven (in the Hispanic version of the game these are the labels of the bottom and top of the diagram). It then becomes possible to understand the Table of Instructions, not as some profoundly meaningful design, but more simply as the internal representation of a metaphysics of hopscotching. In reading Parts One and Two, one hops as directed to one or another fragment of Part Three (but never back and forth, between One and Two). Although there is the strong suspicion that little more than a sense of tedious miscellanea is lost if one omits the two hundred pages of Part Three, its interrelation with the first two parts is a clever allusion to the rhythm of the child's game.

There is another meaning for the game in the structure of the novel and the experiences it represents. Are not the broad outlines of Oliveira's journey also the pattern of the game of hopscotch? Leaving "Earth" (Buenos Aires), he undertakes the journey to "Heaven" (Paris in both a physical and an emotional sense); he attains Heaven through his physical presence in Paris—or we assume that, throughout the first part of the novel, which is told through Oliveira's consciousness (although not consistently in the first person), Paris has been attained physically. There is, however, some doubt as to whether this assumption is strictly true. Considerable internal evidence exists to suggest that Traveler, Oliveira's principal contact after his return to Buenos Aires, is nothing more than his *Doppelgänger*.[5] This doubt raises the matter of the personal autonomy of characters in the contemporary novel. The reader finds them always on the point of ceasing to exist, of merging with faceless nonentities, as though their names were all that made them existentially independent from the reader's point of view. Ironically, the second part of the novel opens with a reference, not to Oliveira, but to the previously unidentified Traveler, who is constantly annoyed by his nickname because he has never traveled outside the country:

He hated the name Traveler because he had never been outside Argentina except for trips over to Montevideo and once up to Asunción in Paraguay, centers that he remembered with sovereign indifference. At the age of forty he was still stuck on the Calle Cachimayo, and the fact that he was a sort of agent

5. This point has been made more than once with reference to a recurring feature of Cortázar's fiction. See René Misha, "Le *Je* et

and jack-of-all-trades for a circus called Las Estrellas gave him no hope whatever of traveling around the world Barnumstyle; the zone of operations of his circus extended from Santa Fe to Carmen de Patagones, with long runs in the capital, La Plata, and Rosario. When Talita, who was a reader of encyclopedias, would get interested in wandering peoples and cultures, Traveler would grumble and speak with insincere praise about a courtyard with geraniums, an army cot, and that no place like home bit. As he sucked on one *mate* after another he would dazzle his wife with his wisdom, but it was obvious that he was trying too hard. When he was asleep he would sometimes come out with words that had to do with uprooting, trips abroad, troubles in customs, and inaccurate alidades. If Talita started to tease him when he woke up, he would start to whack her on the butt, and then they would laugh like crazy and it even seemed that Traveler's betrayal of himself did them both some good. One thing had to be recognized and it was that unlike almost all her other friends, Traveler didn't blame life or fate for the fact that he had been unable to travel everywhere he had wanted to. He would just take a stiff drink of gin and call himself a boob.[6]

This categoric detail about Traveler, who otherwise is only nebulously specified, provides a possible clue to Oliveira's residence in Paris. Such a point depends on other evidence concerning the schizophrenic identity of Oliveira and Traveler. For the moment, it is enough to refer to the prominent opening quotation heading the second part of the novel and to the insistence of the modern novel in denying the autonomy of the individual experience and, therefore, the autonomy of novelistic characters. The great novelists of realism would deplore this circumstance, as many readers still do. But then the understanding of the constitution of human experience has shifted radically enough to make debate on a common ground impossible. We are left with the not unlikely possibility

l'*Autre* chez Cortázar," *Nouvelle revue française*, 12 (1964), 314–22; and, more specifically, Marta Morello-Frosch, "El personaje y su doble en las ficciones de Cortázar," *Revista iberoamericana*, 34 (1968), 323–30; and Anna Marie Taylor, "The 'desdoblamiento' of Oliveira and Traveler in *Rayuela*," *Chasqui*, 1, 3 (1972), 36–40.

6. Ch. 37, p. 219.

that Oliveira not only did not live for a number of years in the Paris of the bohemian's dreams, but also that Oliveira exists only as an independent entity in that dream. When the dream ceases to exist, when he is forced to retrace the squares from Heaven back to Earth (he is obliged to return to Buenos Aires), Oliveira as the focal point of the narrative yields in the second part to a mystifying and inconclusive interplay between one Horacio Oliveira and one Traveler who are probably complementary aspects of the same person.

Vital Games

If there is some likelihood that Oliveira's residence in Paris is to be understood as ideal rather than actual, can we speak of hopscotch as an objective correlative of a journey that is spiritual rather than physical? We have already observed how the apparent triviality of the novel —a highly poetic triviality appropriate to the anxieties of mankind—ultimately comes off as a mockery of the Parisian ideal/idyll. Heaven is, for Oliveira, in the end nothing more than the dreary mirror of his rootless and frustrated existence in Buenos Aires. Seen through the lens of the novel's language, which is not only Spanish instead of Parisian French[7] but also Argentine Spanish instead of the artificial international standard affected by many writers when they place their novels outside their own country, Paris emerges as little more than a locale with particular names rather than *the* Paris of Western aspirations.

7. In many passages, French is presumably the *koine* of a group of miscellaneous nationality (Ch. 15, for example). Yet the Spanish in which these dialogues are presented is as Argentine as the Spanish that is spoken in the second part of the novel, which is set in Buenos Aires. That is to say, although from the point of view of external "truth," Spanish and French are alternated by the characters in Part One, Cortázar's representation of their dialogue in Spanish does nothing to reflect that fact. For example, he could use the international second-person familiar *tú* when French is being spoken and the Argentine *vos* when Spanish is the language. Thus, there is no attempt at verisimilitude as far as language differences are concerned. This fact, although perhaps insignificant, may be related to any nonreality of Oliveira's Paris adventure.

The contrast between the Paris of *Hopscotch* and that of Hemingway's *Moveable Feast* (also 1963) is revealing. If we contrast Oliveira, trying so desperately to find the Paris of spiritual identification, with the autobiographical Hemingway of *A Moveable Feast,* the chasm between what Paris was felt to represent for the intellectual exiles of the twenties and what it can never be for the more pathetic waif of the sixties and seventies becomes evident. The title of Hemingway's work refers to that Paris which is the state of mind, the moveable feast, which an earlier generation thought it had captured, but which can no longer be even a dream to modern man. It is not so much an attack on French culture per se as it is an abstract perspective on the ideal of a city which in Latin America remains strongly synonymous with the intellectual and spiritual goals of Western man. His sense that these goals are either bankrupt or at best irrelevant to his more acute sense of alienation renders the ideal of Paris equally bankrupt, irrelevant.

This misapprehension is precisely why Oliveira's wanderings in the first half of the novel are so absurd: not so much because he is a shallow fool (which he unmistakably is), but because his ideal quite frankly does not exist. Something else may exist in its place, but Oliveira is incapable of grasping that "something else" in his idealistic nearsightedness. To this extent, the game hopscotch has several intrinsic correlations with aspects of the novel's story and structure. But in the end it best represents the infantile wish that Paris be what it cannot be, to which Oliveira clings so tenaciously. Meanwhile, he hops from one square to another, always missing aim with his lagger, never able to reach his nonexistent Heaven.

I have commented that, in its extrinsic pattern, *Hopscotch* is not a *Divine Comedy.* This casual allusion is not without some importance, for Cortázar's novel, along with its schematic pattern and its preoccupation with several possible versions of the journey from Earth to Heaven, also portrays the quest for an ideal woman figure. In the place of Beatrice we have La Maga [the Magician], an

Uruguayan woman with whom Oliveira has a casual but deeply felt liaison in Paris. At one point he loses her, she disappears, and the retrospective first half of the novel is a cry of anguish that she return. Through an extensive series of flashbacks in Oliveira's consciousness, La Maga becomes a truer human ideal than he can ever understand. Oliveira can love only partially, and in the end he is unable to hold on to her; she abandons him, appalled at his stupidity and selfishness. Oliveira searches for her while things, places, events, take on, in the true fashion of the new novel, an inner, private meaning associated with the lover's now-dead relationship. Paris is transformed by Oliveira's aching memory into projections of his liaison with La Maga. The reader perceives an ironic tension between the Paris that Oliveira remembers that he came to discover—the cafés, the galleries, the lectures, the bohemian life of sustained philosophic argument—and the Paris of the delicate and sensitive La Maga, whose truly fabulous sense of the wonderment of life has vanished with her.

Oliveira's quest after La Maga is his *idée fixe* in the first as well as the second half of the novel. Talita, Traveler's wife, becomes a surrogate for La Maga in Buenos Aires. But there is the strong probability that Talita and La Maga are one and the same, that perhaps neither ever existed autonomously, and that the woman whom Oliveira needs so desperately is just as much a creation of his fantasy as his unique capacity for suffering as a man:

And that's how I had met La Maga, who was my witness and my spy without being aware of it; and the irritation of thinking about all this and knowing that since it was always easier to think than to be, that in my case the *ergo* of the expression was not *ergo* or anything at all like it so that we used to go along the Left Bank and La Maga, without knowing she was my spy and my witness, would be amazed at how much I knew about things like literature and cool jazz, which were great mysteries for her. And I felt antagonism for all these things when I was with La Maga, for we loved each other in a sort of dialectic of magnet and iron filings, attack and defense, handball and wall. I suppose La Maga had her notions about me and she must have thought I had been healed of my prejudices or that I was coming over to hers, more and more lighthearted and poetic. In the midst of this precarious happiness, this false truce, I held out my hand and touched the tangled ball of yarn which is Paris, its infinite material all wrapped up around itself, the precipitate of its atmosphere falling on its windows and forming images of clouds and garrets.[8]

In the end, the objective existence of any of these characters, who possess symbolic value in terms of Oliveira's spiritual needs as an intranscendent figure of Everyman, is as unimportant as the objective existence of Oliveira as the protagonist of *Hopscotch*. After all, we are not seeking documentary history in the novel, but only the validity of the experiences given narrative representation. The discussion of objective vs psychotically imagined existence for the characters around Oliveira can be important only if it reveals something about Oliveira. We do come to understand that here is a mediocre and basically selfish man who is nevertheless paradigmatic of mankind. He is Everyman in his dogged necessity to create ideals for himself, to create games that comfort him with their illusory correspondence to the Divine Plan, and in his insistence in pursuing these ideals and these games to justify the trivial chaos that overwhelms each of us. Within this context, La Maga, either as an ideal of pure fantasy or as just another bohemian with more sense and sensitivity than Oliveira, emerges as his most transcendent and therefore his most destructive ideal.

The opening sentence of the novel, which is as crucial as Dante's initial verse, sets the mood for the entire novel: "Would I find La Maga?"[9] The English translation resolves the ambiguity of the original. In Spanish the opening sentence is vague as to whether the narrator is speaking about Oliveira ("Would *he*") or whether Oliveira is

8. Ch. 2, p. 13.
9. Ch. 1, p. 3.

speaking about himself ("Would *I*").[10] Since Chapter One oscillates between first- and third-person narrative, blurring the distinction of traditional, autonomous, grammatical categories of person, the prominent opening sentence is appropriately ambiguous as to the person who utters it. Yet, whatever the narrative point of view, Oliveira's remains the structural point of view, and we perceive everything through the various levels of his vague consciousness. The narrator's precise identity matters little: This is the contemporary novel's interest in distorting the overly neat compartmentalization of author–character–reader. All that matters is Oliveira and what, in turn, matters to him. Cortázar not only shifts narrative point of view erratically via such hoary devices as introducing two narratives into a single chapter, one to be read in the odd lines, the other to be read in the even lines (Ch. 34). In addition, he exploits the potential ambiguities of Spanish, and the opening sentence is one such ambiguity in which the subject can be either first- or third-person singular. From the outset all that is established is the search for La Maga and her discovery as important to someone (the *me* of the second sentence); the specification of the who or the how of this information is suppressed as supposedly trivial.

Returning to the importance of the quest for La Maga, it becomes obvious in the initial chapters that, like Beatrice, she represents some sort of unique feeling or set of values for Oliveira. La Maga *is* emotion or feeling, totally devoid of any "contamination" by the rational preoccupations that beleaguer the search for tranquility, for ataraxia as Oliveira says, by the exile *philosophes*. La Maga is completely abandoned to her sense of the marvelous and without frustrating inhibitions in what she says, does, or thinks. To their companions she is an engaging but indecipherable entity because of her inability to play the the existential games that fill the long hours of their wait-

10. "¿Encontraría a La Maga?" (p. 15 of the original Spanish edition).

ing for Godot. La Maga gives herself over completely to living, to recalling with a touching and pathetic nostalgia the events of her life, to finding in the present moment some consoling delight or absurdly comical happening. Her life-view leaves Oliveira and the others confounded and irritated. Why can't La Maga contain herself and realize the earnest seriousness of their preoccupations instead of begging for another serving of French fries because those on her plate had flown all over the place through her ineptness with a fork? Oliveira is trapped in an attraction-rejection relationship with the woman. When he is alone with her he can let himself go and perhaps for the first time in his life derive some sense of wonderment from her crazy activities. But their relationship is not easy, and when they are with the group it is apparent that Oliveira aligns himself with the others in deploring what the reader sees as the girl's charming freedom:

La Maga could not possibly have decided to turn that corner of the Rue de Vaugirard at the precise moment in which he, five blocks down the street, decided not to go along the Rue de Buci and headed for the Rue Monsieur-le-Prince for no apparent reason, letting himself go along until suddenly he saw her stopped in front of a shop window, absorbed in the contemplation of a stuffed monkey. Seated in a café they carefully reconstructed their routes, the quick changes, trying to find some telepathic explanation and always failing, and yet they had met in that labyrinth of streets, they almost always met and they laughed wildly, certain of some enriching power. Oliveira was fascinated by La Maga's store of nonsense, her calm disdain for the simplest calculation. What for him had been analysis of probabilities, choice, or simply faith in himself as a dowser, for her was simple chance. "And what if you hadn't met me?" he would ask her. "I don't know, but you're here, you see. . . ." For some reason the answer made the question worthless, it showed the logical basis of ordinary common sense. After that Oliveira would feel better able to resist his bookish prejudices, and paradoxically La Maga would fight off her disdain for scholarly knowledge. Thus they went along, Punch and Judy, attracting each other and repelling, as love must do if it is not to end up as calendar art or a pop tune.[11]

Eventually La Maga leaves Oliveira, vanishing in her sorrowful realization of his selfishness and lack of any real human feeling. Oliveira realizes only after she is gone how much she had taught him about coping with the hideousness of day-to-day living. And of course this is precisely Oliveira's problem: how to make it from one day to the next with enough equanimity of spirit left to derive some enjoyment from the small pleasures life does, after all, hold. The very act of existing is Oliveira's unbearable cross, which is why he has sought refuge in bohemian Paris from his dull but apparently normal middle-class Argentine milieu. The loss of La Maga and his realization of what she had come to mean to him can be viewed only as his final realization of the futility of his escape to Paris and the stupidity of his infantile flight into the never-never land of rebellion against what he inescapably is.

Novelistic Ontology

Cortázar's presentation of the relationship between Oliveira and La Maga, both its details and its significance, is not extraordinarily unusual, despite the thousands of words that have been spent on describing *Hopscotch* as the novel to end the novel as we have known it in the West. It is true that the reader must become accustomed to moving between the main narrative and the interca- lated supplementary passages, although one suspects that he will soon either ignore the latter or include them with little sense of their being out of the ordinary. It is true that the novel is studded with verbal tricks, but then so is seventeenth-century fiction. It is also true that one must become accustomed to the shifting points of view. But since the shifts are not part of an attempt to use several points of view to unlock the "truth" of what has hap- pened, we have no difficulty in following what is simply a linear, although not a psychological, narrative. Perhaps

11. Ch. 6, p. 32.

the most salient "experimental" characteristic of *Hopscotch* is the realization that it is ultimately nonmimetic. It does not pretend to portray a series of "real," "historical," "documentary" events, but is instead a narrative fabric in which "real" form is given to the fantasies of one man's immense and uncontrollable anxieties.

On one level we see the novel's narrative action and the outlining of the characters as the subconscious fantasy of a man who fills the vacuousness of his spiritual turmoil with the world of an immense kaleidoscopic game that becomes, on another level, the strange, sprawling novel that the casual reader experiences. Thus, *Hopscotch* may be rather conventional in its presentation of Oliveira, La Maga, and their relationship and, later, of Traveler, Talita, Oliveira, and their rather pedestrian triangular relationship. Yet, on the level of the reader's personal existential experience, *Hopscotch* promises a pattern of meaning that goes beyond the merely mimetic function the novel has traditionally fulfilled. The world of fiction, rather than being the autonomous universe of the novel and the microcosm of the author–reader's macrocosm, becomes the neurotic fantasy, the imaginative projection of a disturbed soul.

At issue here is the extent to which the apparently mimetic, normal but tacky, world of first Paris and then Buenos Aires is just such a projection of the Oliveira whose consciousness is the novel's dominant perspective. We might say that Oliveira, rather than living accidentally in the Paris and Buenos Aires that *Hopscotch* ostensibly portrays, is the creator, with himself a character, of that world in the existential games of his spiritual agony. Then it would not be difficult to move to a mythic level of novelistic creation and say that Oliveira and his creation are the self-same creation of the novelist in the playing out of his own sufferings. Man is obliged to console himself somehow, and Borges's many stories that deal with creation (for example, "The Circular Ruins") are symbolic representations of man's drive toward imaginative fantasy. The artist achieves this end better through his special creative capacity and through his ability to match his anxiety with that of his readers. Or, put differently, the writer is successful to the extent that his creations are convincing in representing what the reader only unconsciously senses.

It is the author's artistry that makes *Hopscotch* more than the touching story of a nostalgic relationship between two persons, which is destroyed by the obsessions of one. On this level alone the novel would possess a relatively lasting interest for its sensitivity of portrayal in the novelist's ability to make us understand Oliveira although he is not attractive as a person. But the total significance of the story grows if the reader views it, not as just the elaborate figment of Oliveira's troubled imagination, but as the detailed projection of his consciousness. This view holds that how much of the story is "true" is basically unimportant; that part of the story which Oliveira experiences as being subjectively "true" is vitally important. At times we get the story directly from him, at others from an unidentified narrator, who may be Oliveira standing outside himself. Whatever the source, the story invariably comes to us via the focus of his consciousness, his "problem," his troubled person.

Herein, then, lies the particular significance of Cortázar's novel and the justification of its innovative effort. Beneath the superficial pattern of a relatively straightforward story, obscured somewhat by the mostly ironic intercalation of a miscellany of passages, lies another pattern of meaning: a series of games invented with varying degrees of fantasy by a consciousness that is seeking an undefined ideal and a release from his personal anguish. That these games take a number of forms constitutes the richness of the narrative fabric. They are epitomized by the hopscotch and its reference to the symbolic Christian journey from Earth to Heaven: this children's game is, as we have observed, the guiding correlative of the novel. But there are other games that are even more interesting: the game of Left-Bank bohemia, for example, with the goal being an undefined Sartrean Heaven (Oliveira is really quite ludicrously inept in his manipulation of the soul-tingling clichés of "being and non-being").

Perhaps the best demonstration of this game, aside from more incidental details of his relationship with La Maga, is the death of her ailing son, for it is this event that finally drives La Maga away from Oliveira. The group, the Serpent Club, has gathered at La Maga's apartment, where her son lies sick (Chapter 28). La Maga tries to control the rising tone of the discussions so he can sleep. But Oliveira discovers by accident that the boy has died. His decision not to interrupt the party and to deprive the mother of her expression of grief is typical of his egocentric distortions:

Horacio slipped his hand under the sheets, it was a great effort to bring himself to feel Rocamadour's tiny stomach, the cold thighs, there seemed to be a little warmth left farther up, but no, he was so cold. "Fall into the pattern," Horacio thought. "Shout, turn on the light, start the obligatory hustle and bustle. Why?" But maybe, still . . . "Then it means that this instinct is of no use to me, this thing I'm starting to discover from deep down inside of me. If I call out it will be Berthe Trépat all over again, the same stupid attempts, pity. Put the glove on, do what must be done in cases like this. Oh no, that's enough. Why turn on the light and shout if it won't do any good? An actor, a perfect fucking actor. All that can be done is . . ." He heard Gregorovius's glass tinkle against the bottle of *caña*. "Yes, it's quite like *barack*." With a Gauloise in his mouth he struck a match, taking a good look. "You'll wake him up," La Maga said as she put some fresh *yerba mate* in his gourd. Horacio blew the match out brutally. It's a known fact that if the pupils, under a bright light, etc. *Quod erat demonstrandum.* "Like *barack*, but a little less aromatic," Ossip was saying.[12]

Of course when La Maga discovers that Rocamadour has died, her grief is acute and profound; Oliveira is only vaguely irritated. After all, so many great questions were being pursued (we get a verbatim transcript of their sophomoric verbiage) and death, the triumph of the

12. Ch. 28, p. 147.

chthonic unknown, can be considered inconsequential by the *petits philosophes*. Death for them is only the whimpering end, the release from anguish and the need to philosophize. They are utterly incapable of grasping La Maga's grief—like the old man upstairs who, with none of their pretensions to existential commitment, is more honestly angry because the uproar has disturbed his sleep.

End Game

La Maga vanishes soon after her son's death, leaving Oliveira a hastily scribbled letter that the reader never sees. Her disappearance is significant both thematically and structurally. In one sense she vies in Oliveira's subconscious for ascendancy with the "Heaven" goal of his game of hopscotch. Although he thinks Heaven is the consolation of existential philosophy, against his wishes the girl has insidiously supplanted the game. And against his better judgment, he takes more and more delight in her crazinesses. This has been evident from Chapter 2. Only when she is no longer present does Oliveira consciously take stock of his situation, and in mixed sorrow and wounded masculine pride he is able only to mutter that she is sure to return (Chapter 29). On the more abstract level of the novel's structure, La Maga's disappearance triggers the transition from Paris to Buenos Aires. Oliveira has no choice but to recognize that he is inept at the game in Paris when he loses La Maga, the true human spirit, and any hope of self-discovery.

The return to Buenos Aires is a defeat on two fronts, and the man's sanity, which was stable if somewhat artificially alienated in Paris, quickly disintegrates when he is back in his homeland. The bohemian dream has been shattered, and, faced with a national reality which he cannot mythicize, Oliveira goes completely mad, which might be the best possible Heaven for him. In the confusingly ambiguous finale of the novel, with its optional, obligatory, and marginal chapters, it is no surprise that it *appears* that Oliveira leaps from his window in the asylum he is helping to manage and falls to the hopscotch painted on the sidewalk of the courtyard below; he lands on Heaven. The fact that the reader is not certain whether he dies or survives the fall is as unimportant as the biographical status of the characters of the novel. It is the sense, insofar as we can discover it, that matters: Oliveira has finally, lunatically attained fulfillment in the games of existence he has pursued so frantically.

The pursuit becomes frantic in Buenos Aires, whereas it had been only haphazard in Paris. Oliveira's abandonment by La Maga is largely responsible for the intensification of this pursuit. He throws himself headlong into the search for her in France and subsequently in Argentina. He frequently thinks he sees her on the streets of Buenos Aires. He now has a more fixed goal, for the striving for Heaven and the search for the girl become a game in earnest. It would be easy to say that because of this search Oliveira acquires a more profoundly human dimension, both because La Maga is a woman of rare spiritual quality and because his search is a true commitment. But one doubts seriously that the pursuit humanizes Oliveira to any impressive extent. Throughout, he remains the pathetic egoist whose pride rather than soul has been mortally affected by the now unattainable ideal, which he previously treated with such gross indifference.

The idea that Traveler and Oliveira are one, that La Maga and Traveler's wife Talita are also narrative halves of the same person, is not new. Carlos Fuentes recognized this possibility and its meaning for the novel in an earlier essay on *Hopscotch*.[13] For Fuentes, the relationship between the two sides of the same story, *that* side, which is Paris, and *this* side, which is America—Argentina—Buenos Aires, is the complex pattern of dependence on Europe, of flight from the immediate (New World) reality, and of the inability of man to accept what he is rather than to live uselessly off the false promises of Western culture.

---

13. Carlos Fuentes, *La nueva novela hispanoamericana* (México: Joanquín Mortiz, 1969), pp. 67–77. Fuentes's essay was originally published in 1967.

Oliveira's return to Buenos Aires is a tacit agreement with that judgment, and his comical madness, like Don Quixote's, is rooted in native soil. One critical tradition has noted that the true classical essence of tragedy occurs when the individual is confronted with the psychological image of himself in an inevitable moment of self-awareness. Does Horacio Oliveira possess a tragic dimension that, if it does not make him humanly attractive, at least affords him a demented dignity? To the extent that his madness and his questionable suicide are born of self-awareness and the realization that he cannot find release in the childish games of Left-Bank bohemia, then the answer is yes.

Two of the best episodes of the second part of the novel give some support to the foregoing opinion. One episode is the story of the board Oliveira extends from his window, across the street to Talita's, in order for her to send him some *yerba mate*. Talita finally attempts to cross over on the board, and the whole event becomes an irrelevant farce in *tempo lento*, with an abundance of details and faithfully reported dialogue that exasperate the puzzled reader (Chapter 41). Talita, caught in the middle of the precariously suspended plank, subjected to the advice of Oliveira at one end and Traveler at the other, has too obvious a meaning to require belaboring. She is the ideal caught between two halves of the man: romantic Oliveira, who has failed to find the answer in his philosophic grand tour of Europe, and pragmatic Traveler, the circus entrepreneur and later insane asylum administrator, who has never left Argentina. This passage partakes of standard black comedy and would be intolerably tiresome if it were not such a high point in Oliveira's new game of hopscotch, in which ascension toward the Heaven of self-recognition and comforting madness are the final validation of his antics:

"So what?" Traveler said. "Why do I have to play games with you, chum?"

"Games play along all by themselves; you're the one who sticks a pole in the spokes to slow down a wheel."

"A wheel that you invented, if you want to bring that up."

"I don't agree," Oliveira said. "All I did was create the circumstances, as anyone who can understand would see. The game has got to be played clean."

"You sound like a loser, old man."

"It's easy to lose if somebody else is rolling the dice."

"Big shot," Traveler said. "Real gaucho talk."

Talita knew that somehow they were talking about her, and she kept on looking down at the errand-girl, motionless on her chair with her mouth open. "I'd give anything for them to stop arguing," Talita thought. "No matter what they talk about, it's always about me in the end, but that's not what I really mean, still it's almost what I mean." It had occurred to her that it would be very funny to drop the package so that it would fall into the errand-girl's mouth. But she didn't really think it would be funny because she could feel that other bridge stretched out above her, the words that passed back and forth, the laughs, the hot silences.

"It's like a trial," Talita thought. "Like a ritual." [14]

Ceremonies are, to be sure, social or religious rituals whereby man assures himself of the ordered meaning of his existence. That is to say, ceremonies are mere games raised to a more transcendent importance, and for Oliveira qua Talita and Traveler, the games are becoming increasingly important. The narrative proper of the novel concludes with the labyrinth Oliveira constructs in his room with wire and ball bearings to trap Traveler. Obsessed with Talita, whom he now identifies completely with La Maga (or has he finally rid himself of the illusion that the latter existed independently and reintegrated her with "another" man's attractive wife?), Oliveira is certain that Traveler is out to get him and wants to defend himself behind the labyrinth.

The labyrinth is either man's refuge from the unknown beyond his own consciousness, a trap for the unwary who presume to discover what it hides or, more primitively, it is the *ad hoc* creation by man of a symbol of the universe and a symbol of his own mind. To the extent that the labyrinth is a universal archetype, Oliveira's defense net-

14. Ch. 41, p. 248.

work has a little of all the foregoing aspects. It is an ultimate cry of desperation in which Oliveira–Traveler face each other, a contest between segments of a single personality. Traveler attempts unsuccessfully to overcome Oliveira's obsession that he must destroy Traveler in order to preserve the autonomy of psyche that he thinks he has attained. Traveler, the untraveled Argentine, is all that Oliveira is not: easygoing, basically insensitive, thoroughly adjusted to the reality of his creole existence, unconcerned by the Great Questions that send men to Paris and drive them mad. This lack of interest in eternal problems Oliveira cannot accept, and therefore he sets out to trap Traveler, even though they have ostensibly been the greatest of friends; that is to say, they have coexisted in schizophrenic equilibrium. When it becomes evident that Traveler cannot be destroyed and when he advances on Oliveira, either to protect him from falling out the window or to attempt to destroy him in turn, Oliveira falls to the patio and the hopscotch below. Later, Traveler and Talita remark casually as they go to bed:

"Horacio saw La Maga tonight," Talita said. "He saw her in the courtyard, two hours ago, when you were on guard duty."

"Oh," said Traveler, lifting up his shoulders and looking Braille system for his cigarettes. He added a confused phrase that had come out of what he had just been reading.

"I was La Maga," Talita said, snuggling closer to Traveler. "I don't know if you're aware of that."

"Most likely yes."

"It had to happen some time. What surprises me is that he's become so startled by the mixup."

"Oh, you know, Horacio gets something started and then he looks at it with the same look puppies put on when they've taken a crap and stand there amazed looking at it."

"I think it happened the very day we went to meet him at the dock." Talita said. "It's hard to explain, because he didn't even look at me and between the two of you treated me like a dog, with the cat under my arm."

Traveler muttered something unintelligible.

"He had me confused with La Maga," Talita insisted.

Traveler listened to her talk, alluding as all women do to fate, to the inevitable concatenation of events, and he would have preferred for her to shut up but Talita resisted feverishly, squeezed up against him and insisted on telling things, telling herself, and naturally, telling him. Traveler let himself be carried along.[15]

The meaning of this exchange is unclear. Within the foregoing context, it may mean that, like the episode with the board, Oliveira has been playing again, but thank heaven he has had his fun for the night and they can relax until the next episode. Or it may mean that Oliveira the gamesman has receded into Traveler's normal personality and that Talita can inform him now that the game is over and tell him what course his "irregularities" assumed this time. In either case, the conversation is implausibly offhand. Did Oliveira die or was he only hurt? Did/does he exist apart from Traveler? Is/was he only Traveler and Talita's game, an extension of the clever fantasies of the circus sideshow and the pathetic delusion of the insane asylum? Will Oliveira *be* again, or has he finally reached whatever Heaven awaited the final toss of the lagger? The novel as an apparently verisimilar story degenerates quickly at this point, and the reader is hopelessly entangled in the concluding chapters of Part Two, confused by their circular interrelationship with the final optional segments of the third part and the placement of the even less coherent chapters at the end of Part Two, which are missing from the reading directions.

It has been said that *Hopscotch* is a novel for accomplice–readers, for readers who must help make the novel mean something and not sit back to be spoon-fed by an indulgent author. Cortázar's novel is certainly no source of comfort; indeed, it must seem downright perverse to those who read to pass the time. To this extent, the reader can be said to be an accomplice: He must fit together as best he can the pieces of the novel that are presented to him in a highly fragmented fashion. Part of the difficulty arises from readers and critics who miss the novel's many

15. Ch. 55, p. 324.

ironies and take its surface meanings too seriously. It may be a violation of the canon of integralist literary criticism to insist that a work of literature be taken on its own terms, that the novel must be understood as an intentional whole. But in the case of *Hopscotch* one must entertain the notion that a good portion of the novel is pure hoax, designed to mislead or to satisfy certain types of readers. Those who expect mimetic, representational fiction will be led astray in their literal understanding of soul-searching existential fiction and will be satisfied in their word-by-word consideration of the bargain-basement philosophizing in the novel. From this discussion of the novel, Cortázar's particularly insistent ironic manner should be all too evident.

This novel refuses to be conventional, but its alternative conventions are probably self-mocking—mocked to the same degree as the conventions of the "psychological and issues" novel: characters who alternate between their roles as identifiable embodiments of the crises of Western man and their role as interchangeable fixtures in a novelistic structure that plays variations on themes rather than plotting a unified Aristotelian action; a narrative language that moves freely among styles that are essayistic, documentarily colloquial, burlesquely archaic (Oliveira's use of the outmoded slang of his youth), "Barthian" (objective *écriture*; self-conscious literariness), and mockingly autocritical; a narrative voice that alternates between reader-identification and character-identification, with traces of unconcern in identifying with either, especially in the "optional" chapters that present Morelli's novelistic *vade mecum*. Cortázar's irony is, to be sure, far from gratuitous, far from an optional component of his narrative. Irony has become the major technical strategy for the novelist to distance both himself and his reader from the objective structures of the novel, to suggest to the reader that he evaluate critically what the novel can present only ambiguously as though it were a final answer to the enigma of man's mandalalike quest, and, finally, to guarantee the autonomy of his literary structure, which is only with great risk appropriated by the unwary as sacred writ.

And by the same token, those who are convinced of the advent of literature's Armaggedon will greet with misplaced enthusiasm the rightly unrevealed scribblings of Morelli's notebooks, which the Serpent Club intends to enshrine as self-satisfied exegetes. Indeed, Cortázar's next novel will be based on these scribblings. His *62: modelo para armar (62: A Model Kit* [1968]), based on Chapter 62 of *Hopscotch*, makes sense only if we take into account the pomposity and the gobbledy-gook that envelops what is simply a description of *Hopscotch* and most important examples of contemporary fiction. The reader becomes an accomplice in another sense also: He is expected to edit the manuscript judiciously in order to decide for himself not only its meaning but also its application to the delineation of Oliveira and his spiritual torment. He is to determine, too, those parts that are superfluous rubbish. All of it may be rubbish, like Oliveira's existence, or all of it may be pertinent. The significant factor here is that there is enough evidence of Cortázar's *playing* with the novel and with the reader (what, for example, is to be made of Chapter 130 other than ironic irrelevance?) to cast doubt on the integrity of a pat, tight description of the structure of the novel as we have known it. The reading instructions, a literal but unnecessary correlative of the hopscotch, when considered along with the optional chapters, alternate reading schemes, and unaccounted-for chapters, should be warning enough to all but the most pedantic of critics.

Of value in the novel is not the cleverness of the exterior girding—although enough critical attention has been paid to the extrinsic structure of *Hopscotch* to cause doubt about this statement—but rather the internal, nonvisible components of the narrative structure. This inner structure, beyond hopscotch and the other games that may or may not find their objective correlative in the obviously eccentric features of the book, can be discovered only after a careful consideration of Oliveira as the controlling focus. I have not answered conclusively the real aim of the man's search, and I have not resolved categorically the matter of character autonomy. Nor has the issue of narrative independence—Oliveira's, the narrator's, Cortázar's—been laid to rest. I cannot be categorical because the work is deliberately evasive. Cortázar makes overt in *Hopscotch* only the fundamental critical tenet of many knowledgeable readers: that a work has no one, ideal interpretation, not even for the author. It is instead what one makes of it, including what he can reasonably convince others about it. *Hopscotch* in this regard is most innovative in making a virtue out of the ambiguity that holds inevitably for any piece of literature.

Finally, I can say only that it appears that these issues do not and must not matter. They are the rigorously avoided province of some other concerns in literature: the "answer," the "solution," the "resolution," the end and the epilogue and the sequel. Despite all the intriguing questions, *Hopscotch*, at the end of one's reading, is only the outline of a novel. The author has, with phenomenal success, produced as a finished literary product the vague notes for a complete, documented history of the Serpent Group and the Insane Asylum Administration. But then that is all he can do, for Oliveira's existence never rises above a rough outline, and it would be both presumptuous and ludicrous for a novel to pretend to attribute more to so slight a structure. In one of the optional selections that ought to be taken literally because of the melancholic tone that aligns it with the general sense of Oliveira's pilgrimage, we have an ironic epithet for a novel that is purposefully deceptive in both its length and in its extrinsic pretensions:

LIFE as a "commentary" of something else we cannot reach, which is there within reach of the leap we will not take.

Life, a ballet based upon a historical theme, a story based upon a deed that once had been alive, a deed that had lived based upon a real deed.

Life, a photograph of the noumenon, a possession in the shadows (woman, monster?), life, pimp of death, splendid deck of cards, ring of forgotten keys that a pair of palsied hands degrade into a sad game of solitaire.[16]

16. Ch. 104, p. 522.

Chapter Six

ALTERNATIVES TO PROGRESSIVE NARRATIVE
IN THE CONTEMPORARY ARGENTINE NOVEL:
SOME CONSTANTS

... the values of mythification, of the narrative structure and of writing as transparent vehicles of the opacity of the world.[1]

If one takes Julio Cortázar's *Hopscotch* (1963) as the high point of recent Argentine fiction, it is possible to discern a major interest among important writers, both new and established, in structures that represent alternatives to the progressive or developmental narrative such as might be associated with the *Bildungsroman* of Eduardo Mallea (*The Bay of Silence* [1940]) and Sabato's early existential novel, *The Tunnel* (1948).[2] My purpose here is to offer what may be considered some significant varieties of this interest in nonprogressive narrative. All of the titles discussed have appeared within the last few years, although no claim is made for a comprehensive presentation of all that is being done. Buenos Aires, as a major publishing center, is producing more each year than even the most dedicated neophile can keep pace with.[3]

1. Carlos Fuentes, *La nueva novela latinoamericana* (México: Joaquín Mortiz, 1969), p. 20.
2. A much shorter and preliminary outline of this chapter was presented to the Latin American section of the 1970 Annual Meeting of the South Central Modern Language Association. I reviewed in summary fashion a number of the novels mentioned, in *Books Abroad*, 1968–1973; the two novels by Puig were reviewed in *Latin American Literary Review*, 1972 and 1973.
3. Several more general but also more comprehensive overviews are available: Emir Rodríguez Monegal, "The New Latin American Novelists," *TriQuarterly*, Nos. 13–15 (1968–1969), 13–32; Federico Peltzer, "Panorama de la última novelística argentina," *Cuadernos del idioma*, 2, 7 (1967), 53–96; Ángela Dellepiane, "La novela argentina desde 1950 a 1965," *Revista iberoamericana*, 34 (1968), 237–82; David Lagmanovich, "La narrativa argentina de

Two interrelated strands of the interest in nonprogressive narrative may be noted. One is related to variants of the so-called new novel,[4] and the other, by far the more productive, gives new life to stream-of-consciousness modes in portraying man's groping for the farthest frontiers of human experience.

Objective Structures

Although it has not been obvious to all readers, Cortázar's *Hopscotch* is both antiexistential and anti-novel-of-commitment. These characteristics I attempted to reveal in Chapter Five. It is difficult to tell which is more ludicrous: Horacio Oliveira's existential posturings or Morelli's inflated novelistic theory as reported in the fragments of the "dispensible" Part Three. Both are true and valid, but only so in the pathetic irony of the irrelevant Paris-oriented goals they objectify. Thus, when Cortázar published his *62: modelo para armar (62: A Model Kit)*,[5] based ostensibly on the thesis advanced by the venerable Morelli in what was Chapter 62 of *Hopscotch*, the critic's initial orientation could be only cautious skepticism.

On one level Morelli's notes are the epitome of theoretical pretentiousness. They describe in mimetic terms the prototype of a novel based on some new neurological concept of memory and consciousness. Yet on another level, once we brush aside a rhetoric that an Horacio Oliveira would take seriously, we recognize a nucleus descriptive of *62: . . . :* a novel that gives narrative substance, not to the worn ethic of the existential quest for commitment

---

1960 a 1970," *Nueva narrativa hispanoamericana*, 2, 1 (1972), 99–117; Julio Lafforgue, "La narrativa argentina actual," in his *Nueva novela latinoamericana* (Buenos Aires: Paidós, 1969–1972), II, 11–30.

4. The new novel of French inspiration in the fifties has had no significant impact in Argentina, and Abelardo Arias's study is in reality devoted to rather dubious characteristics of one author's work. See his "Orígenes y concordancias argentinos de la 'nueva novela' francesa," *Davar*, No. 100 (1964), 67–71.

5. Buenos Aires: Sudamericana, 1968. Translated from the Spanish by Gregory Rabassa (New York: Pantheon Books, Inc., 1972).

and being, but to our awful presentiment of a pattern of existence laid down by some unknown god and imposed upon but giving order to what we foolishly believe to be the chaos of our lives.

In *Rayuela* Horacio Oliveira destroys himself in his absurd but hilarious attempts to create his own games of existence; he is incapable of realizing that the very nature of his enterprise is impertinent. In *62: . . .* , one of the characters remarks, in a moment of frustration that stems from his struggle to make sense out of the weird pattern of events, that "Sartre's crazy and that we're much more the sum of the acts of others than our own."[6]

In this antiexistential, depersonalized "psychological" novel, Cortázar manages in 269 pages to create a fictional world in which a handful of characters are caught up in a strange pattern of events that are undoubtedly definable in terms of their total experience, which we are unfortunately not permitted to see. They are driven in turn by basic human self-awareness to try to make some sense of this pattern, only to realize that the pattern is beyond their control, that they are merely tokens in its machinations, and that it is best to follow the paths along which they have been channeled without destroying themselves in the futility of seeking answers to the great, transcendent questions. The novel is psychological to the extent that it deals with the reality of the individual on the interior and/or subconscious level of his being, in terms of his frustrations at being unable to use a conscious logic to formulate any justification for a desired, autonomous uniqueness. The inexplicable, unknown game that he is drawn into, the permutability of his supposed uniqueness with the experience of the other "players," all contribute to that exquisite pitch of tension implied by Morelli's notes, in which one's carefully shaped personality threatens to disintegrate into so many neuro-electrical charges. Man is basically a victim of existence, which carries him along through its labyrinths. Although this insight is

---

6. *62: A Model Kit*, p. 257.

certainly not original, representing it in terms of a definitive refutation of existential character autonomy and the grandiloquent ethic of self-realization is. In the place of the latter we have the depersonalized, anticommitment detailing of the *how* of the labyrinth, the perception of which explodes the illusion of individual dominance of circumstance and of man's attempt to thread his way out. The *why* of the existence of the labyrinth and of man's failure to dominate it obviously can be the stuff only of the sentimental novels of an earlier generation.

Cortázar provides direct, objective manifestation of the vital maze of his characters in the use of structural parataxis, which involves the interweaving of several threads of narrative with little regard for their autonomy. Rather than maintaining each thread separate in our perception of the mysterious narrative, the point of view, narrative voice—even character integrity—shift so rapidly that we become enveloped, so to speak, in one tangled skein that can be meant only to represent existence or our sole substantial awareness of it. For both character and reader the result is a sense of event such that, to paraphrase someone's interior monologue, "a mirror of space and a mirror of time had coincided at a point of unbearable and most fleeting reality before it left me alone again with so much intelligence, with so much before and after and so much in front of and in back."[7] A hyperbolic definition of perception, to be sure, but one that, whether or not it is meant to be ironic, may be the only convincing verbalization possible of the nonsubstance of nonevents in which we seek the fleeting importance of our overworked human consciousness.

Set in Paris and with a cast of miscellaneous South-American exiles, Cortázar's most recent novel *El libro de Manuel (Manuel's Book)*[8] is unmistakably reminiscent of *Rayuela*. In the place of that wornout ersatz bohemian Oliveira we have a *Doppelgänger* narrator—both Andrés the participant and the "el que te dije (the one I said)"

7. *62: A Model Kit*, p. 27.
8. Buenos Aires: Sudamericana, 1973.

who is the ironically distanced narrator. And in the place of the tragic La Maga, we have Ludmilla, who preserves all of her forerunner's charmingly zany characteristics but does not turn into *Rayuela*'s symbol of tragic innocence spurned by the anti-hero's self-serving existential agonies. Three generations are represented in *El libro de Manuel*: the narrator's (he identifies himself as passé, from the tango rather than the younger "jerk" generation), the generation of the young revolutionaries who alternate between plans for revolution made over the telephone in a code based on the food market and street guerrillerism and intended to startle the bourgeoise, and, finally, the Manuel of the title, the baby of one of the South American couples, who is passed from hand to hand in those interminable conversations that are a Cortázarian hallmark.

Appearing to lack the (illusorily?) rigid structure of *Rayuela*, *El libro de Manuel* comes off as both sincerely revolutionary in its devastatingly critical approach to hallowed values (and Paris is this time less Oliveira's Left Bank myth and more that nitty-gritty reality of the solid citizens who support De Gaulle and Pompidou and who place these exiles on a level barely above Moroccans and Algerians) and critical in its equally devastating portrayal of revolutionary postures that are a time-consuming *dolce far niente* and an opportunity for clowning farce rather than a deeply held conviction.

Two aspects of the novel stand out in particular. First is Cortázar's magnificently comic control of the Spanish language and the Argentine dialect. Language, beyond being the most creative aspect of the work, is a tool for self-criticism, for criticism of self-important ideologies, and for criticism of self-satisfied bourgeois social values. Structurally, Cortázar attempts to achieve the illusion of a text-in-the-making through the use of the *Doppelgängerei* of the narrator, who early in the work participates in and then later re-creates specific events, and through the intercalation of French newspaper clippings. These clippings are, the introduction alleges, chosen at random during the writing of the novel. They are subjects for comment by the characters as they translate them into Spanish, and in turn, they comment on the actions of those same characters. Furthermore, the clippings become part of a carefully compiled revolutionary baby book for Manuel.

El libro de Manuel may not be as important an event as *Rayuela*, but it is a highly entertaining and serious novel, and much more satisfying than *62: modelo para armar*, for both its language and Cortázar's return to a highly foregrounded *écriture*.

* * *

Although Eduardo Mallea represents the school of the traditional psychological novel, several of his recent titles merit attention as examples of the writer's continuing attempt to renovate his fiction; perhaps the most interesting is *La red (The Network)*.[9]

Since Ovid's time metamorphosis as a literary motif has been used to give external, objective, and symbolic representation to a state or conception of animus. As part of the same tradition, physical transformation is an effective and appropriate punishment of the individual for his spiritual abnormality and transgressions. Mallea's *La red* reveals a reliance on metamorphosis as a dominant narrative format for providing vivid superficial formulation of the psychological aberrations and obsessions that are metonymic of the characters in the majority of the selections. The title refers to (1) the topography of Buenos Aires, anthropomorphized in one series of italicized commentaries; (2) the labyrinthine nature of the human personality in the abstract, as portrayed in the parables and longer narratives that constitute the remaining two types of selections; (3) the structure of the book, organized in adherence to a strict geometric pattern. The three types of selections are distributed into twenty chapters, with an interlude (a relatively longer story) after every fourth chapter; the last segments suggest a circularity reminiscent of the infinite extension of the streets peopled by the

9. Buenos Aires: Sudamericana, 1968.

characters that are given symbolic representation in the main narratives.

La red constitutes Mallea's generally successful attempt to blend his principal preoccupation with the so-called psychological modes of modern fiction with the depersonalized, more figurative orientation of younger writers like Cortázar. Although many of the selections (there are sixty-seven in all) are inane and tired clichés—probably purposefully so—the longer stories are interesting because of Mallea's acute penetration of what is seen as the human psychosis, modified significantly in this work by a humorous irony and the currently fashionable tendency toward a ritualistic, manneristic concentration of formulaic expressions and patterned structures. But the most significant acceptance of antipsychological modes is the personification of Buenos Aires (usually grammatically masculine) as a mysterious and difficult enchantress whose characteristics, as described in twenty connected segments, are meant to correlate with those given in the remaining forty-seven parables and stories. By blurring the lines between animate and inanimate and by choosing to portray the defining psychoses of his characters in terms of objective and therefore inanimate metamorphoses, Mallea's traditional attention to the uniquely individual is modified considerably in the direction of ritualized symbols.

*　　*　　*

Leopoldo Marechal's antepenultimate novel, the hyperbolic and expressionistic *El banquete de Severo Arcángelo* (*The Banquet of Severo Arcángelo* [Severe Archangel]) [10] portrays the enactment of a mock Last Supper, held under the spiritual aegis of a modern fulfillment of the Apocalypse. Ostensibly related to the author by a participant, Marechal's novel is one more perplexing example of his lifelong preoccupation with religious themes and his fascination with man's relationship to religion—his drive to fulfill a desire for transcendence (or at least its promise) and for the comfort of satisfying cosmic systems.

10. Buenos Aires: Sudamericana, 1965.

Significantly, the novel is related in the first person by a man who could epitomize the "lost lamb" motif of religious and existential visions of the human circumstance. Called to the banquet under mysterious arrangements, the narrator enters a marginal world controlled by Arcángelo, a tortured Caligula figure who is in real life an industrialist with an imposing steel empire. Arcángelo now must satisfy in an appropriately tyrannical fashion a new-found desire for cosmic justification. The result is the spectacle of the banquet. Our comprehension is controlled by the observations of the narrator, who is only one of several participants. Each participant has been attracted to the function, which we see in its planning rather than in its enactment, for private and often tragicomic reasons. Thus, while a community comes to exist around the plans for the symbolic event, in reality that event holds a different meaning for each man, locked in the shell of his individual personality and his individual memory and experience.

It is apparent that the banquet fulfills a twin symbology. On one level it is a ritual burlesque of Christianity. The burlesque lies not so much in the reader's grasp of the facile allusions of the event's trappings but rather in the profound intention of its organizers as we come to perceive it. Seriously or otherwise, Arcángelo has set out to re-create the intense and mesmerizing atmosphere that Sunday-school teachers like to attach to biblical times. His guests are pulled into a vortex of heady events that should both detract their attention from the misery of their own private lives as well as impart to them a cathartic sense of apocalyptic fulfillment.

On another level the banquet is symbolical in its implications concerning man's need for such diversion, although certainly one need is satisfaction of man's constant desire for transcendency. Certainly traditional religious fulfillment is dismissed as inadequate if not directly impertinent. Arcángelo's event, then, comes to represent an alternative experience that both meets man's spiritual needs and matches the immediate conditioning of his

place in contemporary society. In this way the prelimi-
naries to the banquet are focused on leading the participants through labyrinths of self-awareness in terms of
their immediate experiences like men trapped in the de-
humanization and demythification caused by modern society. By definition the banquet must be a hyperbolic
utopia that will concentrate man not only on himself but
more insistently on some ideal, any ideal, that will provide self-meaning.

The trappings as well as the banquet reduce the event
to theatricality and depressing farce. One can view the
farce as the extension of Arcángelo's capitalistic background: He is providing a representative segment of the
masses with a carefully chosen opiate that he administers
according to his own program of dosage. Or the farce is
merely the projection or reflection of man's attempts to
create meaning out of nothing. One meaning is as good
as another, which means only that one is as farcical as
the other. When the whole structure collapses, as it is
predestined to do, it leaves behind the rubble of its
pretensions, curious but meaningless in their own tragicomic way.

This rubble constitutes the bulk of the novel. Through
the field of vision of the one participant we see both the
banquet as well as his own intensely personal and yet dis-
jointed involvement with it. One is not satisfied with all
of the implications of this involvement or with an understanding of their meaning. Marechal is prone to a sort of
conceitful metaphysics reminiscent superficially of Roberto Arlt's writings, but oriented less sympathetically in
terms of the unfortunate human experience and more
sardonically in terms of a theologian manqué:

"[In the last analysis] what was the purpose of Severo Arcángelo's undertaking? For himself and for others had he set up
his Banquet along the lines of a last-judgment compulsion?
And this compulsion, did it originate in a premonition of
another cyclical disaster in the history of Man, a disaster
whose immanence demanded the construction of an Ark or
a refuge? I [the author] will not set down the dubious an-

swers that I arrived at that night in my intimate questioning:
I understand that, in line with the wishes of the organizers
of the Banquet as told me by Farías [the narrator and afore-
mentioned participant], the theorem is to be left standing
and open to the inquisitions of the soul."[11]

*   *   *

Antonio di Benedetto, despite a studied provincialism
(he is from Mendoza) that is untypical in Argentine culture, has attracted a solid following for his fiction in
both Argentina[12] and, oddly enough, Germany, where his
works have been published in translation. *Zama*[13] is his
best-known work. It is a novel of many peculiar faces. Set
in some unspecified northern River Plate colonial outpost
during 1790, 1794, and 1799, the novel is told in the first
person by the title hero and is based on what can be described only as a kind of anachronistic existentialism. The
basic premise of the novel, reminiscent of that form of
existential speculation that transforms Christ into an ex-
istentialist, is that don Diego de Zama, a historical non-
entity of overwhelmingly trivial proportions, is of interest
to the modern reader for the "fear and trembling unto
death" that he conceals behind the aggressive mask of the
colonial politician–adventurer.

The function of the first-person narration (and our
"access to it" is perhaps not made clear enough) is to provide a contrast between the external appearance of Zama's
aimless but typically colonial existence as he reports it
and his inner or quasi-conscious assessment of his motivation. These motives include, aside from the "fear and
trembling," a sense of the absurdity of intricate patterns
of social behavior, an awareness of the inescapable amo-
rality of the human soul, and an apprehension of the
complete aimlessness of existence and its frightening
Sisyphean burden.

It would appear that *Zama* is almost a textbook example

11. *El banquete de Severo Arcángelo*, p. 291.
12. See the group project on his work, "Aproximación a la obra
de Antonio di Benedetto," *Nueva crítica*, 1 (1970), 85–104.
13. Buenos Aires: Doble P, 1956.

of the existential novel and therefore deserves no more serious attention than precisely this observation. The characteristic that provides the novel with some distinction is its unity in terms both of its anachronistic focus and the underlying motif of Zama's "actions." This focus can be taken only as a specific illustration of a fundamental universality of human existence: It is not modern man himself who is confused emotionally and spiritually; his confusion is the result of his inability to see himself and his nature clearly—a vision he could achieve by dispensing with the artifice and false transcendency of Western culture. What better setting could be devised for the demonstration of this point than the dying days of the Spanish colonial empire? Zama, although he cannot on one level free himself from the period and institutions that surround him, is able on another level of conscious awareness to consider critically the implications of his usually ridiculous behavior in terms of a complex of momentary social and political conventions.

Because of his nature Zama is trapped by a "waiting," a conviction, to which he clings out of unspoken despair and yet rejects out of bitter awareness, that something better and meaningful awaits him. The German translation, proving that translation often is an act of interpretation, makes this motif explicit: *Und wartet Zama (And Zama Waits).*[14] The objective correlative for this wait is the ship, the link of communication between the Spanish court, the viceregal centers, and the colonial outposts. Zama is always waiting for "his ship," to use the English cliché. It never arrives, and the novel can ultimately be seen as a uniform elaboration of the opening image: Zama contemplating the fresh body of a dead monkey trapped between the pilings of a dock, swept back and forth by the ceaseless currents.

New Psychological Modes

Turning to the second and more productive example of current Argentine interest in nonprogressive narrative

14. Tübingen: Horst Erdman, 1967.

modes, we have many titles from which to choose. Works in this category concern the search for more profound bases of human consciousness than the developmental trajectory of stream-of-consciousness psychology and might include a relatively traditional allegory by Silvina Bullrich, *La creciente (The Flooding)*,[15] the magical realism of José Chudnovsky's *Pueblo pan (People of Bread)*,[16] the pseudoconfessional novel by Manuel Mujica Láinez, *Bomarzo*,[17] the vignettes of violence à la Hemingway in the short stories and novels by Dalmiro Sáenz. The few titles I can discuss here might all be grouped together as narrative essays that focus on the "secret ceremony" of the human soul—to take a phrase from the title of Marco Denevi's charming little classic.[18]

*   *   *

Daniel Moyano, already widely recognized as a powerful voice in the Argentine novel, realizes in his fifth novel, *El oscuro (The Dark One)*,[19] a brilliant series of insights into universal human nature through the fragmentary reconstruction of a trivial but tortured, and therefore engrossing, personality. Realized structurally as a flashback, the work explores from the first-person point of view (his consciousness but not always his voice) a man's unsuccessful attempt to find a defense mechanism that will free him of the burden of a disturbing memory. The Dark One is man's soul—not necessarily Víctor's, the protagonist who constitutes the "controlling consciousness"—but a collection of the souls (particularly his wife's) that he tries to manipulate unjustly in his knowledge of their secrets. His

15. Buenos Aires: Sudamericana, 1967.

16. Buenos Aires: Losada, 1967.

17. Buenos Aires: Sudamericana, 1962. The English translation is also entitled *Bomarzo* (New York: Simon & Schuster, Inc., 1969). I discuss this novel in "The Monstrous in Two Argentine Novels," *Américas*, 24, 2 (1972), 33–36.

18. *Ceremonia secreta*, first published in *Life en español*, December 12 and 26, 1960. Available in book form under the same title, Buenos Aires: Calatayud, 1968. It was made into a movie about 1967 under the title *Secret Ceremony*, with Elizabeth Taylor and Mia Farrow.

19. Buenos Aires: Sudamericana, 1968.

purpose is to justify to himself and to the world the triviality and the meanness of his own soul. That Víctor is a chief of police is no accident. He is obsessed with the conviction that his efforts to discover the weaknesses of others is a service both to them and to the nation. Therefore, he is undoubtedly the embodiment of Moyano's preoccupation with a particular type of individual and with a particular type of limited and ignorant superego that is an unrelenting hallmark of the arrogant self-styled saviors of the world; Argentina has not been excepted of late from their flourish. An external air of conviction and carefully executed power masks an inner self-rejection that can be satisfied only by undermining, by spiritually violating, the dignity of the multitudes whom their "saviors" see as threats to their flimsy autonomy.

Yet, *The Dark One* is far from being a political novel. Rather, it is an exercise in the realization of what we might call a "psychiatric myth"—an archetypal truth indicative of the spiritual malaise of a society or civilization as opposed to the dynamic myths through whose creative force a people seek renovation and continuity. In Moyano's case, what is wrong, what is "sick," is defined in terms of the inseparable narrative strands of Víctor's attempts to penetrate and to destroy the inner souls of his wife and a student–striker as well as through the rhythm of troublesome recollection of trivial events and places that haunt him. These recollections Víctor is never quite able to comprehend, never quite able to grasp because they flow from a humble and healthy love between individuals and from respect for the inviolable autonomy of a man's being. If Víctor feels himself the despised outsider, it is because rejection is the only palpable emotion, the result of his moral sickness, that he can experience. *El oscuro* is an impressive work for its competent manipulation of an unusually narrow consciousness whose disintegration we witness from within in order to attain an understanding beyond Víctor's own pitifully limited comprehension. While avoiding facile political and sociological clichés, Moyano is successful in constructing a vision of an Argentine reality through the consciousness of an individual who is an indicative archetype of that reality.

*   *   *

María Esther de Miguel's novel, *Calamares en su tinta* (*Squid Served in its Own Ink*),[20] is much like a drawn-out tango. The novel's story is little more than an interlude in which the lives of two mature adults intertwine briefly in a love that soothes their aching memories of life. She is a sensitive provincial girl who has experienced the usual oppression of a narrow way of life. He is a refugee from the Nazi horror. The novel is the peeling-away of their Bergsonian memories, and we witness the coming-together of their separate paths and then their painful separation when he acquiesces—against her will—to participate in new trials of war prisoners in Germany. Characteristic of the contemporary novel and its quest for the hidden formulas of a secret ritual, the work suggests as a point of departure the ceremonial phrase, "I murmured: one's memory, wherever you touch it, hurts."[21] Through no fixed point of view (yet perhaps we are dealing with only his point of view) but fragmented into several contrastive levels, the novel pursues a unifying rhythm that probes two isolated memories in accidental conjunction in order to reveal their mutual and coordinate pain. Srta. de Miguel's narrative hypothesis is clear: Despite radically different vital experiences, two individuals can be closely joined in their fundamental human agony. This concept may be only a highly personal variant of the depersonalized, figurative, psychic switching to be found in Cortázar's fiction.

Accommodating a topical reference, the refugee is explicit: We each live in our own spiritual ghetto, from which we must escape if we are to survive. As two who try to flee, the refugee and the provincial girl are compelling in their failure, which is occasioned only in part by the inescapable web of their memory and the engulfing trap of

20. Buenos Aires: Sudamericana, 1968.
21. *Calamares en su tinta*, p. 9.

history. The title underlines the essential triviality of the individual chronicle: Our memories are given shape by the meaning that we attach to the insignificant, such as the secret ceremony recalled by someone's casual suggestion of "squid served in its own ink." In fact, the point of departure for the narrative is the refugee's reading of a novel, *Historia trivial (A Trivial Story)*, that opens the floodgates of memory. As such, the novel is an excellent example of a renewed stream-of-consciousness principle and its attempt to depict memory as a fundamental aspect of the human personality.

*   *   *

Although significant for its expression of an intensely personal dissatisfaction with man's inner redemptive powers, Pedro Orgambide's *El páramo (The Wasteland)*[22] is not an overwhelming success as a novel. Nevertheless, it does manifest the author's attempt to work out a serious expression of human experience. In addition, it possesses a marginal importance for its provincial setting—like Antonio di Benedetto, Daniel Moyano, and Dalmiro Sáenz, Orgambide is not tied to Buenos Aires. In fact, it is obvious that the setting for the novel, the hostile southern stretches of Argentina, is intended as a conceitful pathetic fallacy that runs through the novel. The "wasteland" is alternately a neonaturalistic setting that brutalizes man's soul, a correlative of the degrading meanness of existence in general and in Argentina specifically (an Argentina never quite able to live by her own patriotic illusions), and the soul of the individual who must realize the futility of seeking an intellectual and an emotional solution to his existential anguish.

The novel is a retrospective narration by a doctor who leaves the city to practice in this hostile setting. His choice of assignment is determined through a combination of professional idealism and a desire to seek a simpler existence than the capital offers in order to "find himself," in the Western humanistic sense. As a doctor he is allowed

22. Buenos Aires: G. Dávalos/D. C. Hernández, 1965.

to see more of the life of the town than another might, and he is also provided with a personal crisis between his professional and his personal personalities. The doctor *topos* is familiar to American readers. As the vanguard at a certain time of the new developments in science and allied areas, the medical professional is easily the symbol of an alternative to the superstitious and closed existence of the common man and the society made in his image.

Pablo, the narrator, recounts his experiences in the unidentified provincial town as he evolves from an outsider who merely intends to use the town as the means to an end into an outsider who yet is caught up inextricably in the web of existence of that town. On various levels, but especially on that of the Swiss family with whom he boards and whose daughter he eventually marries, Pablo discovers that life possesses a secret and horrible rhythm from which he cannot escape and which he is ultimately forced to acknowledge. He does not understand this rhythm; the choice of a first-person narration is significant in suggesting that comprehension is less important than simple recognition and acceptance of an unknown pattern that the individual can do little to modify. Aside from unfavorable allusions to national problems, symbolized by the abandonment of large segments of the national health system and the population they are meant to serve, the novel is neonaturalistic in suggesting a close and predetermined relationship between man, his telluric circumstance, and his depressing society. Within this context, self-conscious persons such as Pablo are doomed to spiritual anguish for their inability to adjust to the reality of existence on the one hand and to their realization of the bankruptcy of humanistic ideals on the other. The result, in Pablo's case, is a prophet manqué who can only call attention to his own miserable example. He must resign himself to merely chronicling his terrible realization that he is not the free agent and the humanitarian he had believed himself to be. Little by little he is forced to participate in an expiatory ritual of existence designed and executed by unknown forces. His particular tragedy, materialized narratively in his failure to "do anything" about his wife, who dies by literal or figurative suicide, is to be obliged to realize his ineffectiveness and to be deprived of the innocent consolation of the simpleminded or of those who are totally committed to a prophetic ideal such as Marxism.

Although Orgambide's novel is unsatisfactory on several accounts—its ambivalence between facile sentimentality and a mature exploration of the problems involved, and perhaps an overinsistence on the obvious symbology of the wasteland and on the doctor *topos*—it is clearly a narrative that attempts to cope with the anguish generated in man's soul. His agony flows from his puzzled realization that life is a wasteland that must be populated with experience and that it is also a ritual pattern of events that he can neither rise above nor justify.

*   *   *

Manuel Puig's first novel, *La traición de Rita Hayworth (Betrayed by Rita Hayworth)*,[23] has been hailed by Rodríguez Monegal as one of the most important Latin-American novels of the sixties.[24] The writer's second novel, *Boquitas pintadas (Painted Little Mouths)*,[25] may be as important as his first. Despite its superficial catchiness, the novel represents an intriguing follow-up of Puig's qualities as a novelist demonstrated in the earlier work. Subtitled a *folletín* (pamphlet; the reference to the late-nineteenth-century practice of publishing a novel serially, one chapter at a time), the work as a whole reads like the all-too-familiar script of a serialized soap opera of the thirties and forties. In addition, each chapter is headed by a quotation from one of the hoary tangos by Alfredo Le Pera, associated with that pop figure par excellence, Car-

23. Buenos Aires: Jorge Álvarez, 1968. The English translation is by Suzanne Jill Levine (New York: E.P. Dutton & Co., Inc., 1971).

24. Rodríguez Monegal, "The New Latin American Novel," *Books Abroad*, 44 (1970), 45–50, pp. 49–50 in particular.

25. Buenos Aires: Sudamericana, 1969. Translated by Suzanne Jill Levine as *Heartbreak Tango, a Serial* (New York: E. P. Dutton & Co., Inc., 1974).

los Gardel (whose works have also enjoyed a profitable nostalgic renaissance). Thus, the surface of the work—the narrative proper—is concerned with the gray anguish of the Argentine lower middle classes, with the trivial emptiness of routine existence, and with the pitiful attempts by individuals to achieve some level of emotional satisfaction. These are, to be sure, many of the dominant concerns of the tangos of the period; hence the propriety of the Le Pera excerpts. As Puig affirms in an advertising blurb, his novel is deliberately written for popular acceptance, and one can easily recognize it as being accessible to a spectrum of readers beyond the sophisticates who can be the only audience of a Vargas Llosa.

However, if we examine more closely what Puig may be attempting to do, we find that, beginning with the almost *de rigueur* fragmentation of narrative chronology, his focus is decidedly antipsychological, antipersonal autonomy, and antinaturalistic, despite a certain amount of verisimilitude of tone and language. In the contemporary Latin-American novel, whether one confronts the exuberant fantasies of García Márquez or the depressingly humorless mythographies of Vargas Llosa, he cannot escape the realization of the new novel's dictum that individuals as such are insignificant and that human personality as an abstract generality must be the stuff of the novel because it alone provides the opportunity to say—and to perceive— a truth that is universally valid concerning the subliminal, unapprehended human experience. Normal contemplation cannot provide access to such levels, and it is just such an access which the antipersonalist novel is designed to provide (like Julio Cortázar's *62: A Model Kit*). In Puig's novel, narrative chronology from the outset confuses and blurs the lines of autonomy. The bleak uniformity of tone in the portrayal of emotions, no matter how they are dressed up superficially in terms of moral good and evil, contributes strikingly to the presence of an experience more forcefully than does the multiplicity of conflicting and complementing, interacting and growing personalities of a more naturalistic fiction.

In one sense Puig's novel is the validation of a popular suspicion that the scandalous successes of the soap opera derive, not from the baseness of taste to which it appeals, but from the fundamental validity of a uniform humanity upon which its scripts are based. Puig has, on one hand, some way to go in order to defend his novel against those guardians of the virtue of the modern novel who would insist that it must be difficult and inaccessible to all but the most intense of readers, that it must, in short, be self-consciously a work of art in the best of the vanguard tradition. On the other hand, Puig's work is undeniably interesting. Like the tango, it is unashamedly sentimental, but with a sentimentality that is presented from the cold, cruel point of view of one who knows that it is a pathetic defense mechanism against some basic human truths. For one example, the story of Orpheus would have made a good tango. In the focus of both the tango and the soap opera, as seen in *Boquitas pintadas*, and in an interpretive recreation of those basic human truths, it would be absurd to deny that we are not in the presence of one modern manifestation of myth. Any putative simplicity about the novel is both deceptive and illusory. The complex narrative line, a form of narrative parataxis which goes beyond the multiple but facile narrative threads of the sprawling soap opera or the novel of panoramic realism, reinforces, to be sure, the sense of mythic proportions that go beyond the gray misery of individual destinies. But at the same time, no matter how popular or proletarian the novel may appear to be on the surface, the essential and significant inner complexity of *Boquitas pintadas*, like that of *La traición de Rita Hayworth*, bespeaks the true artistic dimensions of Puig's novel.

One of Manuel Puig's enduring contributions to the new Latin-American novel is, therefore, the brilliant possibility of pop-art forms. Along with García Márquez, Puig has turned away from the dense expressionistic structures of Cortázar, Fuentes, and Vargas Llosa toward a narrative that is dominated by an omniscient teller and a story that is, at least superficially, intelligible to a large audience. In his first two novels, Puig used as the framework for his narrative the American cinema of the thirties and forties (*La traición de Rita Hayworth*) and the Argentine radio soap opera of the thirties (*Boquitas pintadas*). In *The Buenos Aires Affair* (its original Spanish title),[26] the framework is the detective novel, and the story involves psychopathic behavior.

But unlike an American practitioner of the genre like Ross Macdonald, for whom the detective novel is an existential literary form, Puig continues his previous practice of vulgarizing the story while at the same time respecting with harsh seriousness the human elements that lie behind the activities of his characters. Thus, the novel moves back and forth between overt parody (each chapter is prefaced by a segment of dialogue taken from an old movie; the dialogue prefigures the action of the chapter) and serious psychological portrayal. Even the serious part approaches parody as Puig uses motifs that today can only be called pop-Freudianism (for example, the implied reasons for the psychopath's sexual irregularities).

Clearly, Puig is not interested in writing a detective novel simply to provide entertainment, and, while there is an element of surprise, there is really no mystery for the reader to solve. Rather, the mystery lies in the complexities of human emotion. Like Puig's earlier novels, this one stresses violence, both the innate violence of the individual as well as the unchecked violence of our contemporary social milieu, as man's synecdochic sin. In this sense, Puig diverges from those contemporary writers (perhaps Fuentes or Donoso) for whom man's violence is an inescapable force with which he must come to terms.

Affair is pervaded by a rampant sexuality that has only recently become possible in Argentine publications; some may consider it excessive. (A few months after publication it was, in fact, banned as obscene.) But aside from Puig's taking good advantage of the opportunity to give a truly adequate clinical portrayal of psychopathic violence, his

26. Buenos Aires: Sudamericana, 1973.

novel reveals a sustained control of form in its use of multiple narrative techniques and in the finely achieved atmosphere of reader alienation. Puig combines this atmosphere with his pop forms to prevent sentimentalizing and facile identifications.

Conclusion

The foregoing comments on some recent examples of contemporary Argentine fiction do not pretend to constitute a complete narrative itinerary. The shared element that justifies bringing these works together in this discussion is their eschewal of progressive modes of fiction in which character and plot delineation is essentially based on linear comprehension, on a developmental comprehension in the reader. Although some of these works may be superficially progressive in the historical sense of narrative facts, all are characterized by an interest in deeper aspects of human experience. These aspects—so a novelistic metatheory would assert—are not accessible via already traditional psychological modes that assume the autonomy of the personality and character development. Depersonalization and role-switching, fetishistic metonymy, the secret validating ceremony, the ritualistic reenactment of a single experience in an attempt to cross the ultimate threshold of human experience—all of these are cardinal points in a conception of human experience that attempts in its fragmentary, often deliberately annoying and unsatisfactory manner to uncover the most basic patterns and underlying forms of the universal state.

These patterns and forms may reveal man's decay and may reveal the absurd and hidden impoverishment of his spirit, but, unfortunately or otherwise, the novelist seems to imply that they are the materials of life and its representations. The novelist, in his acceptance of an artistic imperative, has found in the type of fiction discussed in this chapter the most appropriate representation, the most appropriate narrative mimesis, for his current vision.

Bibliography

Bibliographies

Diccionario de la literatura latinoamericana. Argentina. Washington, D. C.: Unión Panamericana, 1960–1961.

Foster, David William, and Virginia Ramos Foster, *Research Guide to Argentine Literature.* Metuchen, N. J.: Scarecrow Press, 1970.

Orgambide, Pedro G., and Roberto Yahni. *Enciclopedia de la literatura argentina.* Buenos Aires: Editorial Sudamericana, 1970.

Argentine Novel

Alonso, Fernando, and Arturo Rezzano. *Novela y sociedad argentinas.* Buenos Aires: Paidós, 1971.

Arrieta, Rafael Alberto. *Historia de la literatura argentina.* Buenos Aires: Peuser, 1958–1960.

Dellepiane, Ángela. "La novela argentina desde 1950 a 1965." *Revista iberoamericana,* 34 (1968), 237–82.

García, Germán. *La novela argentina, un itinerario.* Buenos Aires: Editorial Sudamericana, 1952.

Ghiano, Juan Carlos. *Constantes de la novela argentina.* Buenos Aires: Raigal, 1953.

———. *La novela argentina contemporánea, 1940–1960.* Buenos Aires: Ministerio de Educación y Culto, Dirección General de Relaciones Culturales, 1964.

———. *Testimonio de la novela argentina.* Buenos Aires: Leviatán, 1956.

Jitrik, Noé. *Seis novelistas argentinos de la nueva promoción.* Mendoza, Arg.: Biblioteca Pública General San Martín, 1959.

Lafforgue, Jorge. "La narrativa argentina actual." In his *Nueva novela latinoamericana* (Buenos Aires: Paidós, 1969–1972), II, 11–30.

Lichtblau, Myron I. *The Argentine Novel in the Nineteenth Century.* New York: The Hispanic Institute in the United States, 1959.

Peltzer, Federico. "Panorama de la última novelística argentina." *Cuadernos de idioma*, 2, 7 (1967), 53–96.

Pezzoni, Enrique. "Transgresión y normalización en la narrativa argentina contemporánea." *Revista de Occidente*, No. 100 (1971), 172–91.

Plá, Roger. *Proposiciones (novela nueva y narrativa argentina)*. Buenos Aires: Biblioteca, 1969.

Portantiero, Juan Carlos. *Realismo y realidad en la narrativa argentina*. Buenos Aires: Procyón, 1961.

Rojas, Ricardo. *Historia de la literatura argentina . . . .* Buenos Aires: Editorial Kraft, 1957.

Viñas, David. *Literatura argentina y realidad política*. Buenos Aires: Jorge Álvarez, 1964. Published in a greatly revised form as *Literatura argentina y realidad política: de Sarmiento a Cortázar*. Buenos Aires: Siglo Veinte, 1971.

Roberto Arlt

Becco, Horacio Jorge, and Oscar Masotta. *Roberto Arlt [guía bibliográfica]*. Buenos Aires: Universidad Nacional de Buenos Aires, Facultad de Filosofía y Letras, 1959.

Corelli, Albino D. "El pensamiento rebelde de Roberto Arlt." *Universidad* [Santa Fe], No. 70 (1967), 49–60.

Etchenique, Nira. *Roberto Arlt*. Buenos Aires: La Mandrágora, 1962.

Giordano, Jaime. "El espacio en la narrativa de Roberto Arlt." *Nueva narrativa hispanoamericana*, 2, 2 (1972), 119–48.

———. "Roberto Arlt o la metafísica del siervo." *Atenea*, 45 (1968), 73–104.

González Lanuza, Eduardo. *Roberto Arlt*. Buenos Aires: Centro Editor de América Latina, 1971.

Gostautas, Stasys. "La evasión de la ciudad en las novelas de Roberto Arlt." *Revista iberoamericana*, No. 80 (1972), 441–62.

Larra, Raúl. *Roberto Arlt, el torturado*; 2a ed. Buenos Aires: Quetzal, 1962[?].

Maldavsky, David. *Las crisis en la narrativa de Roberto Arlt*. Buenos Aires: Escuela, 1968.

Masotta, Oscar. *Sexo y traición en Roberto Arlt*. Buenos Aires: Jorge Álvarez, 1965.

Núñez, Ángel. *La obra narrativa de Roberto Arlt*. Buenos Aires: Nova, 1968.

Pérez Martín, Norma. "Angustia metafísica en la obra de Roberto Arlt." *Universidad* [Santa Fe], No. 53 (1962), 41–57.

Piccini, Mabel. " 'Los siete locos' de Roberto Arlt: un momento de la realidad argentina." *Hispanófila*, No. 40 (1970), 29–43.

Prieto, Adolfo. "La fantasía y lo fantástico en Roberto Arlt." *Boletín de literaturas hispánicas*, 5 (1963), 5–18.

Sebrelli, Juan José. "Inocencia y culpabilidad de Roberto Arlt." *Sur*, No. 223 (1953), 109–19.

Eduardo Mallea

Becco, Horacio Jorge. *Eduardo Mallea [guía bibliográfica]*. Buenos Aires: Universidad de Buenos Aires, Facultad de Filosofía y Letras, 1959.

Chapman, G. Arnold. "Terms of Spiritual Isolation in Eduardo Mallea." *Modern Language Forum*, 37 (1952), 21–27.

Concha, Jaime. "Eduardo Mallea en su fase inicial." *Anales de la Universidad de Chile*, No. 135 (1965), 71–107.

Dudgeon, Patrick. *Eduardo Mallea: a Personal Study of His Works*. Buenos Aires: Agonía, 1949.

Flint, J. M. "The Expression of Isolation: Notes on Mallea's Stylistic Technique." *Bulletin of Hispanic Studies*, 44 (1967), 203–9.

———. "Rasgos comunes en algunos de los personajes de Eduardo Mallea." *Ibero-romania*, 1 (1969), 340–45.

Gillessen, Herbert. *Themen, Bilder und Motive in Werke Eduardo Malleas*. Geneva: Droz, 1966.

Grieben, Carlos F. *Eduardo Mallea*. Buenos Aires: Ministerio de Educación y Cultura, 1961.

Hughes, John B. "Arte y sentido ritual de los cuentos y novelas cortas de Eduardo Mallea." *Revista de la Universidad de Buenos Aires*, 3a época, 5 (1960), 192–212.

Lewald, H. Ernest. "Mallea's Theme in *La bahía de silencio*." *Hispania*, 40 (1957), 176–78.

Lichtblau, Myron I. *El arte estilístico de Eduardo Mallea*. Buenos Aires: Juan Goyanarte, 1967.

———. "El concepto del tiempo en las obras de Eduardo Mallea." *Humanitas* [Nuevo León], 3 (1962), 299–314.

———. "Rasgos estilísticos en algunas novelas de Eduardo Mallea." *Revista iberoamericana*, 24 (1959), 117–25.

Montserrat, Santiago. "Eduardo Mallea y la Argentina profunda." *Sur*, No. 123 (1945), 72–83.

Morsella, Astur. *Eduardo Mallea*. Buenos Aires: MAC-CO, 1957.

Petersen, Fred. "Notes on Mallea's Definition of Argentina." *Hispania*, 45 (1962), 621–24.

Pinkerton, Marjorie J. "Eduardo Mallea: suplemento a una bibliografía." *Revista iberoamericana*, 30 (1964), 319–23.

Polt, John H. R. "Algunos símbolos de Eduardo Mallea: Mallea y Hawthorne." *Revista hispánica moderna*, 26 (1960), 96–101.

————. *The Writings of Eduardo Mallea*. Berkeley: University of California Press, 1959.

Rivelli, Carmen. *Eduardo Mallea: la continuidad temática de su obra*. New York: Las Américas, 1969.

Rodríguez Monegal, Emir. "Eduardo Mallea visible e invisible." In his *El juicio de los parricidas* (Buenos Aires: Deucalión, 1956), pp. 29–54.

Shaw, Donald L. "Narrative Technique in Mallea's *La bahía de silencio*." *Symposium*, 20 (1966), 50–55.

Ernesto Sabato

Avellaneda, Andrés. "Novela e ideología en 'Sobre héroes y tumbas' de Ernesto Sábato." *Nuevos Aires*, No. 7 (1972), 55–71.

Beuchat, Cecilia. "Psicoanálisis y Argentina en una novela de Ernesto Sábato." *Taller de letras*, No. 1 (1971), 38–43.

Castellanos, Carmelina de. "Dos personajes de una novela argentina." *Cuadernos hispanoamericanos*, No. 232 (1969), 149–60.

Cersósimo, Emilse Beatriz. *"Sobre héroes y tumbas": de los caracteres a la metafísica*. Buenos Aires: Editorial Sudamericana, 1972.

Coddou, Marcelo. "La teoría del ser nacional argentino en *Sobre héroes y tumbas*." *Atenea*, 45 (1968), 57–71.

Correa, María Angélica. *Genio y figura de Ernesto Sábato*. Buenos Aires: Editorial Universitaria de Buenos Aires, 1972.

Dellepiane, Ángela B. "Del barroco y las modernas técnicas en Ernesto Sábato." *Revista interamericana de bibliografía*, 15 (1965), 226–50.

————. *Ernesto Sábato, el hombre y su obra (ensayo de inter-*

pretación y análisis literario). New York: Las Américas, 1968.

Eyzaguirre, Luis B. " 'Rayuela', 'Sobre héroes y tumbas', 'El astillero': búsqueda de la identidad individual en la novela hispanoamericana contemporánea." *Nueva narrativa hispanoamericana,* 2, 2 (1972), 101–18.

Foster, David William. "The Integral Role of 'El informe sobre ciegos' in Sábato's *Sobre héroes y tumbas." Romance Notes,* 14 (1972), 44–48.

Giacoman, Helmy F., ed. *Homenaje a Ernesto Sábato: variaciones interpretativas en torno a su obra.* Long Island City, N. Y.: Las Américas, 1973.

————. *Los personajes de Sábato.* Buenos Aires: Editorial Emecé, 1972.

Holzapfel, Tamara. "El 'Informe sobre ciegos' o el optimismo de la voluntad." *Revista iberoamericana,* 38 (1972), 95–103.

————. "Metaphysical Revolt in Ernesto Sábato's *Sobre héroes y tumbas." Hispania,* 52 (1969), 857–63.

————. "*Sobre héroes y tumbas,* novela del siglo." *Revista iberoamericana,* 34 (1968), 117–21.

Lipp, Solomon. "Ernesto Sábato: síntoma de una época." *Journal of Inter-American Studies,* 18 (1966), 142–55.

Lorenz, Günter W. "Ernesto Sábato . . . ." In his *Dialog mit Lateinamerika* . . . . (Tübingen: Horst Erdmann, 1970), pp. 39–131.

Ludmer, Iris Josefina. "Ernesto Sábato y un testimonio del fracaso." *Boletín de literaturas hispánicas,* 5 (1963), 83–100.

Martínez, Z. Nelly. "Fernando Vidal Olmos y el surrealismo: una conversación con Ernesto Sábato." *Sin nombre,* 2, 3 (1972), 60–64.

————. "El 'Informe sobre ciegos' y Fernando Olmos, poeta vidente." *Revista iberoamericana,* 38 (1972), 627–39.

Rodríguez Monegal, Emir. "Por una novela novelesca y metafísica." *Mundo nuevo,* No. 5 (1966), 5–21.

Souza, Raymond D. "Fernando as Hero in Sábato's 'Sobre héroes y tumbas'." *Hispania,* 55 (1972), 241–46.

Julio Cortázar

Alegría, Fernando. "*Rayuela:* o el orden del caos." In his *Literatura y revolución* (México: Fondo de Cultura Económica, 1971), pp. 126–46.

Amícola, José. *Sobre Cortázar*. Buenos Aires: Escuela, 1969.

Arellano, Sonia. *Tres eslabones en la narrativa de Cortázar*. Santiago de Chile: Ed. del Pacífico, 1972.

Aronne Amestoy, Linda. *Cortázar: la novela mandala*. Buenos Aires: Fernando García Cambeiro, 1972.

Barrenechea, Ana María. "La estructura de *Rayuela*, de Julio Cortázar." In Julio Lafforgue, *Nueva novela latinomericana* (Buenos Aires: Paidós, 1969–1972), II, 222–47.

——. "*Rayuela*, una búsqueda a patir de cero." *Sur*, No. 288 (1964), 69–73.

Benedetti, Mario. "Julio Cortázar, un narrador para lectores cómplices." In his *Letras del continente mestizo* (Montevideo: Editorial Arca, 1967), pp. 58–76.

Copeland, John G. "Las imágenes de *Rayuela*." *Revista iberoamericana*, 33 (1967), 85–104.

Curutchet, Juan Carlos. *Julio Cortázar o la crítica de la razón pragmática*. Madrid: Editorial Nacional, 1972.

Dellepiane, Ángela. "Algunas consideraciones acerca del lenguaje en Cortázar." *Sin nombre*, 2, 2 (1971), 24–35.

Donni de Miranda, Nélida. "Notas sobre la lengua de Cortázar." *Boletín de literaturas hispánicas*, No. 6 (1966), 71–83.

Eyzaguirre, Luis B. " 'Rayuela', 'Sobre héroes y tumbas' y 'El astillero': búsqueda de la identidad individual en la novela contemporánea." *Nueva narrativa hispanoamericana*, 2, 2 (1972), 101–18.

Figueroa, Esperanza. "Guía para el lector de *Rayuela*." *Revista iberoamericana*, 32 (1966), 261–66.

Filer, Malva E. *Los mundos de Julio Cortázar*. New York: Las Américas, 1970.

García Canclini, Néstor. *Cortázar: una antropología poética*. Buenos Aires: Nova, 1968.

Giacoman, Helmy F., ed. *Homenaje a Julio Cortázar; variaciones interpretativas en torno a su obra*. Long Island City, N. Y.: Las Américas, 1972.

Giordano, Enrique. "Algunas aproximaciones a *Rayuela*, de Julio Cortázar, a través de la dinámica del juego." In Helmy F. Giacoman, ed., *Homenaje . . .*, q.v., pp. 95–129.

Gullón, Germán. "La retórica de Cortázar en *Rayuela*." *Insula*, No. 299 (1971), 13.

Harss, Luis, and Barbara Dohmann. "Julio Cortázar, or the

Slap in the Face." In their *Into the Mainstream* (New York: Harper and Row, Publishers, 1967), pp. 206–45.

Irby, James E. "Cortázar's *Hopscotch* and Other Games." *Novel*, 1 (1964), 64–70.

MacAdam, Alfred J. "Cortázar 'novelista'." *Mundo nuevo*, No. 18 (1967), 38–42.

————. " 'Rayuela', de Julio Cortázar: un tipo de análisis estructural." In Ángel Flores and Raúl Silva Cáceres, *La novela hispanoamericana actual* (New York: Las Américas, 1971), pp. 91–119.

————. "La simultaneidad en las novelas de Cortázar." *Revista iberoamericana*, 37 (1971), 667–76.

Morello-Frosch, Marta. "El personaje y su doble en las ficciones de Cortázar." *Revista iberoamericana*, 34 (1968), 323–30.

Ostria González, Manuel. "Concepto e imagen del lector en *Rayuela*." *Chasqui*, 2, 2 (1973), 22–32.

Rein, Mercedes. *Julio Cortázar: el escritor y sus máscaras.* Montevideo: Diaco, 1969.

Sanhueza, Ana M. "Caracterización de los narradores de *Rayuela*." *Revista chilena de literatura*, 1 (1971), 43–57.

Sola, Graciela de. *Julio Cortázar y el hombre nuevo.* Buenos Aires: Editorial Sudamericana, 1968.

Sosnowski, Saúl. *Cortázar, una búsqueda mítica.* Buenos Aires: Ediciones Noé, 1973.

Taylor, Anna Marie. "The 'desdoblamiento' of Oliveira and Traveler in *Rayuela*." *Chasqui*, 1, 3 (1972), 36–40.

David W. Foster presents a concise overview of Argentine narrative from the late nineteenth century to the present. He illustrates his points through analysis of major texts and their roles in the intellectual development of the country.

Foster analyzes structurally four novels by four major Argentine novelists in the twentieth century. Two are from the pre-"new narrative" period (Roberto Arlt and Eduardo Mallea) and two from the "new narrative" boom (Ernesto Sabato and Julio Cortázar). Materials from their works provide evidence of their importance in the national literature.

Brief analyses of the works of Leopoldo Marechal, Antonio di Benedetto, Daniel Moyano, María Esther de Miguel, Pedro Orgambide, and Manuel Puig combine to provide a general characterization of principal forms of the novel in Argentina today.